# Seed Saving

Become a Seed Saving Pro and Master the Art of Harvesting

*(The Basic Techniques for Harvesting, Storing, and Planting to Ensure Fresh Produce)*

**Stephen Herrera**

Published By **Cathy Nedrow**

## Stephen Herrera

All Rights Reserved

*Seed Saving: Become a Seed Saving Pro and Master the Art of Harvesting (The Basic Techniques for Harvesting, Storing, and Planting to Ensure Fresh Produce)*

**ISBN 978-1-7777356-7-8**

No part of this guidebook shall be reproduced in any form without permission in writing from the publisher except in the case of brief quotations embodied in critical articles or reviews.

Legal & Disclaimer

The information contained in this book is not designed to replace or take the place of any form of medicine or professional medical advice. The information in this book has been provided for educational & entertainment purposes only.

The information contained in this book has been compiled from sources deemed reliable, and it is accurate to the best of the Author's knowledge; however, the Author cannot guarantee its accuracy and validity and cannot be held liable for any errors or omissions. Changes are periodically made to this book. You must consult your doctor or get professional medical advice before using any of the suggested remedies, techniques, or information in this book.

Upon using the information contained in this book, you agree to hold harmless the Author from and against any damages, costs, and expenses, including any legal fees potentially resulting from the application of any of the information provided by this guide. This disclaimer applies to any damages or injury caused by the use and application, whether directly or indirectly, of any advice or information presented, whether for breach of contract, tort, negligence, personal injury, criminal intent, or under any other cause of action.

You agree to accept all risks of using the information presented inside this book. You need to consult a professional medical practitioner in order to ensure you are both able and healthy enough to participate in this program.

## Table Of Contents

Chapter 1: Importance Of Seeds And Seed Saving ........................................ 1

Chapter 2: History Of Seed Saving .......... 19

Chapter 3: The Basics Of Seed Saving ..... 39

Chapter 4: Seed Saving Techniques ........ 49

Chapter 5: Storage And Germination ..... 59

Chapter 6: Specific Crops Seed Saving Guides ..................................................... 63

Chapter 7: Planning A Seed Garden ....... 76

Chapter 8: Edible And Nutritious Seeds . 85

Chapter 9: Troubleshooting And Faqs .... 89

Chapter 10: The Magic Of Seed Conservation ........................................... 99

# Chapter 1: Importance Of Seeds And Seed Saving

Seeds are their species' technique of survival. They are a manner via which the embryo's existence can be all but suspended earlier than its rejuvenation for state-of-the-art improvement; even a long time after the natural dad and mom are lengthy gone Plant seeds preserve and resource life They are well-prepared facilities with enough unique meals elements to face up to protracted sieges. Seeds feature vendors for the transfer of recent life from one area to each other by means of the factors, animals, and those. Food for people, animals, and various residing creatures includes seeds. They are wealth.

They are adorable. They feature a place to begin. They are messengers of goodwill, kindness, and assist. The miracle of seeds is countless. They are the focal point of research in man's in no way-finishing quest to understand residing subjects. Although seeds have numerous functions, their primary characteristic is to make certain continued lifestyles. We are fed by using using vegetation. The plants moreover offer food for special animals on the whole planet. However, from wherein do the ones flora come? Plants feed animals and those. These flora develop from seeds.

1.1 Where does a seed come from?

A plant can satisfactory reproduce via seeds. A seed is the begin of a contemporary plant. In the center in their give up end result, fruiting plants frequently produce their seeds. You could likely have observed seeds internal an orange or an apple. Without seeds, there might now not be any vegetation, and there could not be any seeds without plant life, either. As a end result, seeds are crucial to the arena's sustenance, and it's miles critical to take measures to make certain that they may be collected and preserved in a manner that stops the extinction of precise fruit, vegetable, and wildflower instructions. The ripe, mature ovaries of plants are what we name fruits. Bell peppers, tomatoes, cucumbers, eggplants, and green beans are only a few examples of quit end result which can be often flawed for veggies however are in fact fruits. Fruits cover and protect seeds. What, then, is a seed? The seed can be defined due to the fact the embryonic level in the life cycle of the plant. The embryo, endosperm, and seed coat are the 3 primary components of maximum seeds. A root, stem, and one or extra leaves may be positioned inside the embryo of a tiny plant. The nutritive tissue of the seed is known as the endosperm, and it regularly includes a combination of starch, oil, and protein. The seed coat acts as a barrier which can maintain seeds alive for a completely long term. When consuming fleshy surrender quit result, we frequently avoid seeds, however many well-known dry food devices encompass seeds. That includes the majority of tasty legumes, together with peas, beans, lentils, and peanuts. Although a nut is in reality a fruit, at the identical time as we devour our favourite nuts, like cashews, walnuts, filberts, and pecans, we normally eat the seed and toss the fruit (or shell). Despite now not coming from seeds, pine nuts, almonds, and Brazil nuts are all seeds. Some spices, like nutmeg, mustard, and fenugreek, are seeds. Coffee beans and chocolate beans, of our favourite non-legume "beans," are seeds. What about grains like rice, corn, and cereal? Although the majority of what we consume—and almost all the nutritious fee—comes from the seed, technically speaking, grains are seeds which may be fused to the ovary wall, making them stop result. Poppy, flax, and pumpkin seeds are just a few of the well-known seeds.

1.2 Phases of seed improvement

Development of fertilized ovule into a seed takes region after pollination. Even although seeds play a crucial characteristic in a plant's existence cycle and function food for each people and one-of-a-kind animals, we but understand little or no approximately how genes manipulate the development and growth of seeds. Most research has been finished to date at the angiosperm inside the mustard family Arabidopsis thaliana, which has served as a unmarried "version" species. The genes responsible for the ovule and seed development in Arabidopsis have been diagnosed via studies, but it is not feasible to understand how flora got here to have this type of severa range of seed kinds because of the dearth of excellent research concerning masses of plant companies. According to analyze, gymnosperms have more copies of the genes that regulate ovule and seed improvement in spite of getting particularly easy ovule and seed structures in assessment to angiosperms.

1.3 Three critical components of a seed.

The seed is the most vital part of a flowering plant. They produce a new plant. All seeds have a tiny hollow. This hole plays a totally important function in the consumption of minerals, water and oxygen. This approach is needed to break open seeds. This gadget moreover allows in its increase thru the soil into an man or woman plant. Seeds are to be had in numerous sizes, shades, and shapes. They can be wrinkled, winged, spherical or bushy. Until they achieve sufficient sunshine, water, and soil, they'll be dormant. Germination is the approach through which a seed grows proper right into a plant. There are three crucial factors of a seed:

1.Three.1 Seed Coat

The seed coat allows in protecting the inner additives of the seed. Two layers incorporate the seed coat. The outer layer, it in reality is thick, is referred to as the testa. The call of the internal layer is tegmen. The seed is protected from water and sunlight hours with the useful resource of way of the primary layer. It prevents the entry of parasites into the seed and moreover protects the water loss. When the environmental situations aren't favorable, the hard seed coats prevent germination. On some seed coats, a gap referred to as the micropyle may be visible inside the ovule's integument. Additionally, the hilum, this is similar to the naval in human beings and is in which the umbilical cord is established, is obvious.

1.Three.2 Endosperm

This a part of the seed allows in storing the nutrients. In the form of starch, carbohydrates, and proteins, it offers the seed vitamins to manual the embryo at some stage in germination. Sead coat is placed above the endosperm. Until germination, the seeds stay viable with the consumption of nutrients. Endosperm can be ruminated, non-stop, or mealy. A triploid chromosome complement is found in an endosperm. Endosperm makes up a large a part of the seed in corn and special cereals. In seeds together with beans, the endosperm is lacking due to the fact it's far used for the duration of embryo development.

1.Three.Three Embryo

Embryo is the 1/3 and the maximum vital part of the seed. A fertilized egg results in its improvement. Diploid is the choice given to an embryo because of the stated truth. The embryo includes every cell required for its improvement. An embryo is crafted from severa components. The epicotyl, a tiny shoot, is the supply of the whole plant shoot system. During germination, the primary root is the primary to appear. It moreover goes via the choice hypocotyl. It securely anchors the plant to the floor. A radicle is a tiny root of the embryo. The one-of-a-type factors of the embryo are nourished by way of using the cotyledons. It grows out of the earth alongside the seedling as a tiny or fleshy leaf. Protein and starch are the 2 types of meals that it stores. The first leaves to emerge above the floor are the embryonic ones. A fertilized egg outcomes within the improvement of an embryo.

1. Four Seeds containing flora

Flowering vegetation, collectively with angiosperms and gymnosperms, or "naked-seeded" plants like conifers and cycads, are subgroups of spermatophytes, or seed flora. Seeds are a key feature of spermatophytes. Mosses and ferns are a few of flowers that lack seeds. You want to realise that seed vegetation first seemed in the fossil file. Today, they are the most numerous and widespread plant business enterprise on earth. The distinction inside the period and shape of seeds is related to the way of the dispersal mechanism. You may be amazed to understand that simply certainly one of the largest seeds has a length of round twelve inches. Its floating function allows it to cover big distances. There are some seeds that are very small and can't be visible by using the unaided eye. You should use microscopes to view these seeds. They disperse in the environment without issue. Small seeds embryos that aren't actually superior. They have no endosperm.

1.Five A Seed and its competencies

Reproduction effects inside the development of seeds. Moreover, maximum seeds are produced with the resource of sexual reproduction. For the plants which reason them to, seeds have severa makes use of. Important responsibilities consist of embryo feeding, dispersal to a modern-day location, and hibernation in adverse instances. Seeds moreover serve to nourish and defend the embryo or greater younger plant. A seed's number one reason is to make sure the survival of a species. The plant embryo is stored alive through the usage of way of all the realistic systems of the seed until the surroundings is favorable for the germination of the seed similarly to for the seedling to stay to inform the tale. A multitude of things, together with sunlight hours, temperature, and moisture, have an effect on seed germination. A species goes extinct whilst seeds do now not become seedlings that blossom and produce offspring. It might take years, if now not many years, for plant life that thrive in hostile environments to reap the proper surroundings at the manner to assist them to germinate well and really. In those events, seeds lie inactive inside the soil, searching forward to the right timing that could help them to develop and bring flowers. Wildflowers determined in the wilderness serve as an instance of long-lasting seeds. The meals that seeds contain lets in the embryos inner to stay to inform the story germination. Small seeds that sprout speedy and increase at an splendid tempo generally have little endosperm. There is little endosperm in small, rapid-growing and quick-sprouting seeds. Endosperm in big quantities lets in seeds and seedlings to go through beneath unfavorable conditions for extended periods of time. Coconuts make it to coastal areas after floating in the air. Germination can start after pretty an extended duration in such instances. A top quantity of endocarp is furnished through the seed. This enables in the vegetation' right boom.

## 1.6 The Importance of Seed Saving

You can gauge the importance of seed saving from the fact that without seeds, the world can also want to now not be capable of live to inform the story. Seeds are a cornerstone of all of our meals. There are round forty,000 diagnosed plant species in the worldwide. Seeds have the capability to regenerate species, foster biodiversity, and help ecosystems alter to a constantly changing environment. These are the primary reasons why it is vital to keep seeds. Besides, there are more than one reasons which make it necessary to shop seeds. The idea of a seed financial agency became moreover evolved to facilitate the seed-saving technique. The said reality desires that there want to be a severa form of seeds for gratifying nutritional in addition to environmental wishes.

Why preserve seeds?

Even even though now not all plant life produce seeds, those who do often rely upon them to reproduce over the course of severa seasons and years. There is not any denying the reality that seeds are specifically vital. They are rich in carbohydrates and well as proteins. The said factors assist inside the development further to the increase of a plant. Human beings depend distinctly on legumes in addition to cereals. Some examples of seeds are wheat, barley, maize, and rice. How many bowls of rice, cobs of corn and loaves of bread do you consume consistent with week? In addition, an entire lot of the herbal animals in our vicinity consume regularly culmination and their seeds. For example, nearby plant seeds from Banksia, Dryandra, and Eucalyptus offer a massive a part of the meals for masses parrots. Additionally, there are a whole lot of bugs and mammals that consume seeds, like local mice.

Importance of seed saving for early farmers

The legacy, cultures, further to histories of all the ones who have taken care of the ones valuable flora in advance than us need to be preserved, which means that we must preserve our seeds. We may want to now not have meals with out seeds, and early farmers knew that with the resource of choosing seeds from the most critical and greatest flowers within the agricultural land, they may boom every the yield of their harvests and the equal vintage of their produce. We are lucky to have an extraordinary cornucopia of vegetables and give up give up result, with sun shades and flavors that excite the senses and captivate the minds of culinary experts, thanks to the efforts of those early farmers who had been basically the number one plant breeders. By preserving the efforts of these early farmers, we seed savers pay tribute to their hard artwork and determination. Every seed that has been conserved includes the records of each gardener who has ever grown that cultivar and each grower who has ever engaged in this holy dedication of cultivation. And in the identical manner that we generally have a tendency to the ones flora, assembly their requirements just so they will hold to stay, they, in flip, provide us the meals we want to maintain to stay. This together useful interaction maintains via the seed and into the subsequent season after harvest.

Seed saving boosts the functionality of your lawn.

While the blessings of growing personal food are widely known, seed renovation is a manner which no longer many human beings are aware of. Moreover, with the aid of manner of saving seeds, you could revolutionize the usage of your garden. Indigenous agencies from everywhere in the international have engaged in this holy ritual, which is important for maintaining crop variety. It additionally allows in boosting taste. You can also increase the dietary values even as making edition less complicated. Saving seeds encourages environmental care and fosters a clearer statistics of the supply of our food. Because plants are more suitable to the nearby environment at the same time as seed protection is completed locally, it performs an crucial role in withstanding climate alternate. It lets in you in masses of techniques. You do not ought to shop big capital to keep seeds. However, you can ought to build up understanding and analyze techniques in case you are interested in this career.

Importance of Seed saving for gardeners, homesteaders and permaculture farmers

The workout of collecting seeds in addition to storing them for future use is called "seed saving." Rarely do the farmers of the triumphing global indulge within the interest of saving seeds. However, permaculture farmers, homesteaders, and gardeners are keen on it. People plan seed changing activities and meet collectively to alternate saved seeds in severa locations.

If the plant that you use for financial savings seeds is a plant which has been planted thru the usage of a hybrid seed with patenting rights, then this isn't always deemed a prison interest. A paper needs to be signed via the farmers for that reason, promising to apply genetically changed seeds without a doubt as soon as once they determine to shop for them. Then, it'd be a criminal offense to accumulate and hold seeds from this crop. By growing the plant kinds that may be exchanged and stored, seed producers are presently aiming to provide farmers extra alternatives. A splendid understanding to have is the potential to keep seeds, particularly if you experience farming and need to rely on the produce of your lawn. It lets in you to expand healthful plant life and create seeds whose first-rate is exquisite. This can be completed with out counting on distinctive assets. But seed renovation offers various benefits even if you're a out of doors grower at domestic. Saving seeds permits you to:

In addition to developing your lawn's variety, seed saving also allows in saving capital.

Sharing and maintaining seeds permits your lawn grow to be extra numerous at the same time as moreover saving you coins. You do not should take permission for seed saving. Moreover, buying seeds thru seed exchanges and libraries is a long way a great deal much less costly than shopping for seeds from retail seed corporations.

Seed saving allows you in developing and enhancing the precise kinds of plants that you like

You can broaden your chosen flower and vegetable sorts on a every twelve months basis with the aid of storing your seed. Additionally, in case you use the flowers which can be appropriate in top notch for saving seeds, then your plants gets better over time. The very last results is a seed strain that is ideally fitted to the microclimate and garden quarter on your unique location.

## Chapter 2: History Of Seed Saving

Saving seeds is a conventional exercise that dates lower returned hundreds of years, specifically in Indigenous agencies that depend upon plants for cultural and social similarly to meals features. It has been and stays a critical lifeline for the protection of cultures, surroundings and meals safety, further to being an investment in future harvests. However, business agriculture has witnessed a decline of ninety 3% in seed kinds at some point of the past century. The ownership titles to a massive a part of the world's seeds are currently owned with the beneficial aid of status quo agencies and monopolies of agrochemical agencies.

## 2.1 Natural ancient past and Seed Preservation

In order to hold our natural history, seed conservation is vital. Perhaps the most large environmental hassle confronting Western Australia is the dearth of ecological range. The Phytophthora cinnamomi dieback infection is idea to have an impact on a big a part of the vegetation within the species-rich heathlands and on the coastal plains. Dryland salinity is a similarly, nearly insurmountable hazard in the Wheatbelt. The integrity of the plant businesses is also at chance from weed invasion and habitat fragmentation due to ancient and ongoing elimination of nearby flowers, mining, and incorrect fireplace regimes. Seed collections which may be saved for a quick to a long term help maintain neighborhood plant species from going extinct. For the regeneration of bushland or the rehabilitation of degraded landscapes, a number of seed species can be used. When essential, seed from precise species may be used for reintroduction and recovery into managed habitats. This is crucial to the preservation of genetic variety. The burden on wild populations can be lessened with the useful resource of the usage of seeds to boom seed orchards from which greater seed collections can be collected. The cloth from seeds and seedlings can also be applied in clinical studies on the biology of the seed, conservation genetics, and illness susceptibility, presenting facts in order to help our efforts for on-the-floor control and conservation.

2.2 Seeds in the beyond

The records of seeds took a dramatic turn within the center of the 19th century as some of government-primarily based definitely institutions, institutions, and programs were established that discouraged not unusual people from keeping their non-public seeds. When the united states Supreme Court dominated in 1980 that dwelling matters and the genetic fabric contained in them might be patentable, it located an give up to those sports and made seed saving unlawful from patented flora. Studies advocate that near seventy five% of plant species have been out of location because of the commercialization and patentability of seeds, similarly to know-how and cultural practices. Food structures that be afflicted by a lack of variety come to be at risk of fall apart. When agriculture have turn out to be an employer, it compelled farmers to increase their volumes in order that extra sales may be generated. The surroundings changed into compromised and unnoticed because of this aspect. Soil out of vicinity its awesome, and the general fitness of people modified into furthermore affected. Moreover, plants and fauna become additionally hit drastically due to the additives which were used to acquire the said goal. As a end result, seeds' production and distribution inside the United States have been performed via a massive style of farmers who have been now not professionals. Industrial seeds have now changed peasant seeds, and the phrase used to explain the farmers' manner of seed processing. Following the choice of a higher courtroom docket, which grow to be taken within the yr 1980, farmers may moreover need to not store seeds. The Plant Variety Protection Act of 1970 gave businesses a certificates of ownership of seeds. Nowadays, most seed breeding takes place at public institutions or business labs, and organizations are generating seeds that can be with out trouble grown. The yield of those vegetation is immoderate, but they may be used handiest as fast as. As a surrender result of this, farmers can buy new seeds every year. Corteva, BASF, Bayer, and ChemChina are the four corporations that own the maximum worldwide seed deliver. Typically, customers of Corteva and Bayer are required to sign contracts that forbid them from maintaining seeds so that you can exchange them or resow them. This could be a criminal offense in phrases of intellectual assets. Currently, agriculture is owned thru large industries. They revel in the monopoly on this company and are doing more damage to the agency and people than to serve it in an ethical and expert way.

2.Three Indigenous Seed Saving and Seed Sovereignty

In Indigenous communities, seed maintaining have become not unusual exercise till the closing 200 years. Seed keepers in the ones corporations had been chargeable for informing their successors approximately the farming and seed-saving manner. There are as many styles of the flowers as there are of the folklore and cultures that surround them. The acts of folks that save seeds additionally remodel them into historians who tell about those items to their children. A farmer's proper to conserve, use, trade, and sell their very very own seeds is known as seed sovereignty. We can pass within the path of seed sovereignty with the beneficial aid of using seed rematriation. The technique facilitating the skip returned of seeds to in which it belongs has been diagnosed well, and people are the use of it for the hobby of humans and their kid's meals protection. It is an intergenerational motion led thru Indigenous girls who have historically been the guardians of seeds. Rematriation is crucial due to the fact the locals have been forcibly uprooted from their homes and meals sources at some level within the colonial era of the sixteenth century. Along with the effects of forced integration, it is also idea that fine data regarding seed saving and its importance for humanity does not exist anymore.

2.Four History of seed saving and its importance as regards to manner of existence

Even no matter the truth that seeds have the functionality to actually reproduce and grow, human beings were freely gathering, cultivating, maintaining, changing, and spreading them for over 10,000 years. By maintaining crop variety, enhancing taste and nutrients, and selling seed variation to the environment wherein they may be cultivated, seed savers have stimulated agriculture. For human beings, seeds have moreover carried out a massive cultural characteristic with the useful resource of preserving memories and connections to preceding generations. However, because of organization dominance and the weather catastrophe, the ancient beyond of seed saving has significantly modified over the last hundred years.

2.Five Seed saving in current-day statistics

European settlers short found that their crops had been unsuited to the climate of what may want to in the long run come to be the usa after arriving in the Americas. The colonizers became to nearby flora as their plants failed in those absolutely tremendous soils and situations. Europeans started out out seed-saving to create a worthwhile crop series via pressured trade with neighborhood tribes. The US government created an agricultural-targeted patent office using those flowers and countless more that have been accumulated from everywhere in the international. In

1862, the USDA have become legally primarily based, which advanced seed collection, distribution, and propagation. The US authorities supplied over 1.1 billion seed packets to farmers so they could boom and adapt to outstanding climates. When the personal vicinity found out there has been room for boom, seed distribution started out out to modify. The American Seed Trade Association (ASTA) have turn out to be based in 1883 to foster commercial enterprise ties inside the seed area. In 1924, this business enterprise succeeded in persuading the federal authorities to give up the scheme of gifting away unfastened seeds. Patents and intellectual assets rights have been created, in addition consolidating organisation manage over the seed enterprise and making those groups untouchable from an financial and political attitude. The considerable records of conventional seed saving and the social and cultural significance of seeds have been irreversibly altered even as it became illegal for human beings to conserve the majority of seeds owned via businesses. The 4 largest agricultural businesses in the worldwide presently manage more than sixty seven% of the area's seeds, together with Bayer (which obtained Monsanto in 2018), Corteva Agriscience, Sinochem, and BASF.

## 2.6 Seed saving in the present world

Today, if you stroll proper right into a lawn maintain, the bulk of the seeds you see are in all likelihood owned thru manner of the form of multinational agencies. They maximum possibly get hold of insecticide, fungicide, and possibly even genetic alternate treatments. Pesticides also can be essential for the increase of those seeds. Given the shortage of alternatives, retaining seeds is the nice flow you may do for the health of your self, your garden, and the surroundings. Seeds which have been cultivated and saved for your specific vicinity for at least one season are said to be locally tailored. These seeds gather records from their environment, at the side of unique weather patterns, kinds of soil, length of seasons, neighborhood pests, and extra.

These adjustments boom the productivity of your lawn and get rid of the want for chemical inputs like pesticides and fertilizers. Plants turn out to be greater dependable thru responding to their environment through maintaining seeds every yr. Purchased seeds, rather, lack any genetic or natural connection to the environment. For meals protection and resilience, it's far essential to store community seeds that thrive in your particular environment. In slight of the contemporary-day climate catastrophe, unpredictable weather styles, and a deteriorating food tool, that is relatively crucial.

2.7 Seed saving and the characteristic of network

Many culmination and grains may be planted with the resource of a farmer or gardener. You can collect the ones seeds and maintain them for the following 12 months with the aid of the usage of growing a welcoming surroundings for seeds to breed. All of the

DNA and vital initial strength sources for a seed to develop right right into a plant are present inside the seed. It lets in you to preserve developing that particular species of plant. Gardeners and farmers can test with new forms of the plant life they growth that won't be available in supermarkets and lawn centers way to seed saving and the groups that paintings to do the challenge. By retaining seeds, farmers and gardeners can bypass on heirloom seeds to future generations, retaining meals life-style. By venture this activity, farmers and gardeners can also additionally find out about the genetic range of plants, collect their capability as growers, and engage with others thru shared interests. In Appalachia, there are many sorts of beans, however each holler develops its very personal bean. It is normal with the beneficial resource of the sun's real mind-set in that holler, the soil, the weathered rocks, and the human beings, families, and generations who decided to consume the components through the years. It is constantly converting and has the capability to grow to be greater nutritious as well as resilient. At the the front lines of climate disaster are farming and seed maintenance. We have the hazard to reduce our climate influences at the equal time as concurrently strengthening our food gadget in the face of uncertainty with the resource of cultivating greens locally that would adapt to climate consequences. Similar to the case for eating regionally grown food, the case for nearby seeds emphasizes growing relationships amongst buddies, boosting nearby economies, and advancing social justice. Without community, a neighborhood seed motion can not exist. The seed library is one of the primary models for communal seed conservation and sharing. The public can borrow or trade seeds from seed libraries. Their collections are often obtained through offers from friends and close by seed companies committed to sharing their understanding and talents. The taking of seeds on the start of the season and the returning of seeds after harvest should be balanced for this gadget to paintings efficaciously. In the long time, this strengthens connections among businesses and advances seed version. One of the simplest and best techniques for having a green lawn is seed protection. It encourages communal involvement, environmental obligation, and an escape from the global economic system. Additionally, all and sundry is able to doing it.

2.Eight Community Connections with the beneficial aid of sharing records and changing seeds

Through seed swaps and exclusive sports, seed saving offers the threat to bring together relationships in the network. The relationships assist breeders. By gaining knowledge of awesome folks that [seed save] on your community and sharing with them, seed saving and groups shine. Sharing promotes variety, and there are frequently some sorts which can be content cloth to be grown there. There is a lot of information to be received via those sorts of discussions for definitely all people who desires to begin. Hearing about the beans or corn which have been farmed through manner of a specific family for a long time creates a stronger bond. Some households have the ability to hold seed sorts for many years. An opportunity for self-reliance is supplied through the usage of way of seeds that have been grown for a specific valley. Seed conservation contributes to the place's resilience and the survival of the unbiased way of life. We are conscious that this know-how stays held with the aid of people in southern Appalachia who are nonetheless alive, along with their households and their seeds. They preserve heirloom seeds, which is probably seeds passed down from own family to circle of relatives or network preceding to 1950 and have by no means been bought or offered. Communities and the land are reconnected thru seed saving. Growers are lacking out if every body is handiest shopping for seeds. We are missing out on range and the opportunity for humans to have interaction in deep skip-cultural interactions and form bonds with others, despite the reality that their political evaluations are noticeably distinct. By committing to a few component from your community, you may take your region and rework your courting with it. One can connect to the community and the land at places like seed swaps. The seeds are firmly hooked up and emerge as particular to that lawn and that region. You want to start retaining seeds no longer because of the fact you could pinnacle off a large freezer but due to the truth you can maintain relationships with those gardens as well as locations. Connections created at seed swaps are beneficial for way of life and history in addition to information. A new farmer could make masses-wanted first-hand connections with pals who proportion their pastimes and have been stewarding and traumatic for generations through replacing seeds and records.

2.Nine Seed Bank and its significance in Seed Saving

Thus, a seed monetary agency is a type of monetary organization of genes and is defined as an area wherein seeds are stored so that you can preserve genetic range. By amassing severa seed kinds and keeping them in particularly designed buildings or boxes known as seed banks, we're able to boom the threat of plant species' survival. The concept of a seed bank is similar to a monetary institution wherein someone deposits cash. It is because of the fact that seeds can be deposited and stored correctly in seed banks. A lot of nations have seed banks. There are more than 1,seven hundred of them international, ranging in duration from small to massive. The Svalbard Global Seed Vault, typically referred to as the Doomsday Vault, is one in each of the biggest. It is hidden on a mountainside on an island to the north of the Arctic Circle. Although you do now not need ice all round you to maintain seeds nicely as long as you have got a normal temperature of -20°C with low oxygen further to low moisture degrees, the bloodless, dry activities on this region of the world are fantastic for keeping seeds feasible. You can keep an entire lot of seeds and the genetic form of plants that is contained internal them in a very little vicinity manner to seed banks, which provide a totally green technique of doing so. While a few seed banks also can preserve a restricted choice of seeds, others might also exceptional preserve seeds community to the particular place. While some especially preserve seeds of dangerous plant life or weeds, others reputation on easy food flora like wheat, rice, apples and potatoes. It can be difficult to determine which seeds to save. Even with regards to capsules, a plant that we do now not presently use frequently can also flip out to have some aspect we will require within the destiny. When you go through in thoughts that simplest 20 primary plants account for nearly all of the area's meals, it's miles even extra important to preserve a giant form of seed types in case one or extra of these vital genetic assets are wiped out through a brand new pest, infection, or modifications in our weather. The functionality of seeds to stay possible for hundreds of years is an fantastic fact which may be a supply of motivation for all the ones walking for seeds and their upkeep. It is discouraging to recognise that most of the plant species that were in use inside the final century aren't being grown in these days's global. Seed banks provide an superb preference for keeping that historic and cultural cost. It is because of the fact it is able to be taken into consideration as seed libraries which may be capable of containing large statistics about the evolution strategies of flora. It additionally permits in preventing the loss associated with genetic range in uncommon plant species. A majority of seed banks contain seeds that may be used for research geared towards delivering gadgets to the general public. That is why those seed banks also are funded via public. Genes are often required thru plant breeders for growing yield, overcoming disease resistance, boosting drought tolerance, and enhancing the dietary extraordinary of flowers utilized in agriculture. So by way of way of manner of safeguarding this small however important useful resource, seed banks motive to supply precious service to the area. Due to a non-prevent growth in weather change, many vegetation have end up at risk of extinction, that may therefore pave the manner for a global meals disaster. The international populace explosion has additionally contributed to an boom in intake of food that exceeds manufacturing.

## Chapter 3: The Basics Of Seed Saving

In order to understand the fundamentals of seed saving, one have to have a exquisite information of the lifestyles cycles of plant life and seeds, forms of seeds, self-pollinating flora, open-pollinated vegetation, pass-pollinating vegetation and hybrid seeds.

three.1 Understanding Seed Life cycles

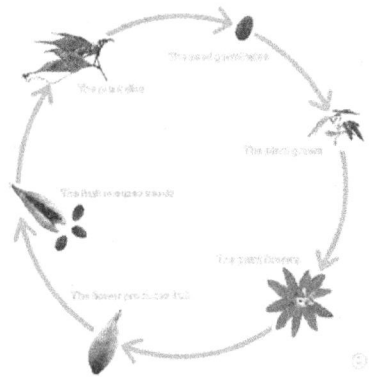

The lifestyles of a plant starts offevolved offevolved offevolved as a seed. Germination of seed is discovered with the beneficial resource of the growth of a modern day plant. Subsequently, plant life are produced with the aid of manner of manner of the mature plant. These flora fertilize and result in the manufacturing of seeds in a fruit. The forestall of the plant does now not imply the stop of the seeds. The seeds live which over again start the device of germination and manufacturing of a contemporary plant. The existence cycles of numerous flowers and seeds are:

Steps that have to be taken sooner or later of the seed-saving tool

Seeds which is probably perennial seeds can be harvested next to the blooming of vegetation. Ensure that there aren't any petals, too. The following steps should be discovered:

The flower head need to be lessen with the useful resource of the use of a knife or scissors.

The seeds which have ripened need to be collected from the pinnacle of the flower.

Then take a piece of paper that has been waxed and placed the seeds on it.

A minimum of 7 days have to receive to seeds for drying.

The seeds need to be cleaned via getting rid of pods or husks.

The seeds want to be positioned in a container. The seeds want to be sealed and saved in a area. It need to then be established a place this is dry and funky.

The seeds need to be sown in spring. They may be planted with brilliant ease.

Monocarpic

They can produce seeds only one time in their lifetime. However, they broaden to mature plant life after a number of years. The Talipot Palm has a existence span of around 60 years or more. It then produces vegetation and seeds after which dies.

three.2 Types of seeds

There are styles of seeds. These are:

Monocotyledonous Seeds

These seeds embody a unmarried cotyledon. They emerge from the seeds on germination. Rice is an instance of this shape of shape of seed.

Dicotyledonous Seeds

These seeds embody cotyledons. They moreover emerge from the seeds on germination. Tomato is an instance of this type of form of seed.

three.Three Understanding Self-Pollinating and Cross-Pollinating Plants

The act of moving pollen takes region from anther. It then movements to the stigma of the same or a wonderful flower. This technique is known as pollination. This kind of pollination takes location in angiosperms. Pollination in gymnosperms includes the motion of pollen from cone this is male to the cone this is female. The pollen germinates the immediate the transfer takes area. The pollen tube is created as a stop result similarly to the sperm. This allows inside the egg's fertilization.

Self-Pollination and Cross-Pollination

There are types of pollination. These are bypass-pollination and self-pollination. Transfer of the pollen from its anther to the stigma of the equal flower or a few other flower on the same plant is known as self-pollination. Some flowers, collectively with lettuce, peas, beans, tomatoes, and peppers, self-pollinate. The handiest technique to start seed safety is with self-pollinated cultivars. When the stamen further to carpel mature on the equal time and are located absolutely so the pollen may additionally moreover pick out the stigma of the flower, self-pollination happens. The plant does now not should make any funding in this mode of pollination so one can provide nectar and pollen as nourishment for pollinators. If you choose out to keep tomato seed, plant the flowers as a long way away from the opportunity tomatoes as you can to reduce the opportunity of crossing. Cross-pollination takes place while a transfer of pollen from a flower's anther takes region. But this transfer is completed on the identical time as the pollen reaches the sigma of a unique flower. Brassicas, corn, carrots, beets, squash, cucumbers, and melons are examples of cross-pollinated plant life that depend upon pollen from precise plants to generate healthy seeds. Garden pea self-pollination and go-pollination help trends switch from one technology to the subsequent, in step with medical studies. The plants grown in recent times are the impact of plant breeding, which makes use of synthetic selection to create the cultivars which may be grown nowadays.

3.Four Open-Pollinated vs. Hybrid Seeds

Generation after technology, the actual plant can be produced via seed from open-pollinated sorts. The offspring due to two excellent determine types' pass is called a hybrid variety. The equal hybrid plant will not be made out of seed stored from a hybrid, but alternatively a plant with a few genetic additives of every.

3.Five Seed Maturity and Viability

Let us first communicate seed maturity and then viability:

Seed Maturity

Unripe seeds are contained in a difficult, fleshy, inexperienced fruit (pod) that is each white, green, or tender, white or green. The seedpod dries up, turns white or brown, and in the end splits to release the mature, ripe seeds, which first turn brown or green and grow a difficult defensive. The plant expends a number of electricity on seed manufacturing. The plant might not have enough energy to complete the tool if it's far useless or loss of life. You in all likelihood won't be able to gain seeds from reduce plants because of this. The seedpod need to stay affixed to the parent plant till the seeds are fully matured in order for the plant with a purpose to accumulate meals at the same time because the seeds are growing. The complete approach of seed development—from fertilization to the losing of the ripe seeds—can ultimate for a long time, but seeds which is probably accumulated in advance than that point will not germinate. Make certain the plant has enough water and meals to provide it the strength it wants to offer seeds in case you are inquisitive about accumulating seeds from the vegetation inside the lawn.

Seed Viability

The lifespans of severa seed kinds vary. The amount of seeds which might be even though feasible to increase plants is known as seed viability. While a few seeds can be viable for decades, others may also additionally furthermore handiest do so momentarily. For instance, watermelon and cabbage need to final at least 4 years, despite the fact that parsley and onion seeds first-rate last a 12 months or . While a few vegetation first-rate preserve their unique germination for a few years, others acquire this for masses more. The conventional one-three hundred and sixty five days wonders encompass delphiniums, parsley, parsnip, onions, and larkspur. They may additionally live on a 2nd year, but their energy and germination is probably considerably less. Onion seed from a domestic lawn normally lasts numerous years. Legumes and carrots typically go through three years, squash 4 years, brassicas five years (eggplant, peppers, tomatoes), and lettuce three to 6 years. Use the ones strategies to behavior a germination test to decide your seed's viability.

Arrange ten seeds on a paper towel that has been slightly wet. The seeds will perish if the towel is overly damp.

To prevent it from drying out, roll the paper towel and located it in a zipped plastic bag. On the outside of the bag, write the date & type of seed the usage of a eternal marker.

Also, take be privy to the seed packet's commonplace germination times.

Keep it there for a few days in a warmth environment (above 70 stages). Although maximum seeds do no longer require heaps slight, a warm windowsill can frequently paintings well.

The seeds should be checked after more than one days to discover if they have all started to expand based on the everyday germination period unique at the seed packaging. Check them in 7–10 days if you do no longer already recognize the usual germination fee. They may be visible via the paper towel. In typically, the roots begin to expand first.

The paper towel-wrapped seeds should be eliminated cautiously from the bag once they have started to amplify. Then, unfold the paper to rely the variety of seeds which have germinated.

## Chapter 4: Seed Saving Techniques

Participating inside the technique of herbal desire is referred to as seed saving. Seeds are produced because of pollination. You should no longer pick out the seed till it's miles ripe. Any try to choose the seed earlier than the right time will negatively impact the germination manner of the seed. Farmers had been preserving seeds for an extended. This helps them in growing real styles of greens, herbs, and flowers. This additionally enables the farmers in dealing with their gardens or farms. By utilising cutting-edge techniques and severa equipment, seed wholesalers often store seeds on a huge scale. But there are wonderful techniques to hold seeds. For homesteaders and permaculture gardeners, small-scale seed saving is a treasured expertise that is simple to investigate, a laugh, and profitable. First, we are in a role to inform you approximately the seeds which are clean to shop, and then we're in a position to speak the seed-saving strategies.

four.1 Learn approximately seeds that may be saved easily.

Beans, peas, lettuce, and tomatoes are remarkable for beginners for the cause that they may be self-pollinating flowers. The seeds of those plants can be stored without troubles. However, some of people assume that legumes are the simplest. In addition to being self-pollinating, they will be processed in addition to grown with out issues, and you do now not want many vegetation to often preserve seeds. Let us now research techniques for saving seeds.

Learn to store the seeds of peas and beans.

You ought to utilize the dry method to preserve pea and bean seeds. Let the big bean or pea seeds mature and dry in advance than cracking them open. Because immoderate warmness would possibly harm the seeds, unfold the seeds for drying in an area with remarkable airflow and shade. Seeds may be saved as quickly as they'll be absolutely dry.

Learn saving seeds of lettuce.

The dry technique is a easy manner to preserve lettuce seeds. You must allow flora on the lettuce plant to wilt. The heads of plant life will now turn out to be fluffy and white, much like dandelion flowers. The seeds shall live related to the white fluffy debris' ends if you pull them out. Gently separate the seeds from the white fluff, then place the seeds which can be easy in luggage for storing.

Learn to preserve the seeds of a tomato.

When maintaining tomato seeds, fermentation is the endorsed method. It enhances the probability that the preserved seeds will germinate. To begin with, take the seeds of the tomato out. Then they want to be placed in a jar with any pulp that is though clinging to them. To maintain pests out, the pulp and seeds have to be blanketed with water and positioned a cheesecloth or espresso filter out on top. When the seed has fermented, the pinnacle have to have a layer of mildew. You can now rinse and dry seeds of the tomato. Throw away any seeds and mould which may be though floating, and then wash the seeds with walking water. To get clean tomato seeds, seeds ought to be rubbed and rinsed till the pulp has been washed away. When the seeds of the tomato are honestly dry, unfold them and permit them to dry within the air in advance than storing them.

4.2 Dry and Wet Processing

The technique for storing seeds will in large part rely upon the form of plant getting used. Most of the vegetation that we expand are dry-seeded. However, flowers of greens is probably moist-seeded or dry-seeded. Moreover, super strategies are used for defensive and storing seeds.

Crops which can be moist seeded

Fruit flesh consists of seeds from moist-seeded flora. Wet-seeded fruit-bearing vegetable households of vegetation embody the following :

Eggplants, peppers and tomatoes are individuals of the Solanaceae circle of relatives

The family of Cucurbitaceae, which includes cucumbers, melons, and squash

Crops which is probably dry seeded

Crops with wet seeds have seeds which is probably included via husks and pods. The family of Poaceae, which incorporates wheat, rice, and corn, is one of the vegetable plant families that may be grown from dry seeds. Moreover, the circle of relatives of Brassicaceae, which also consists of kale, mustard, and cabbage, is dry-seeded, along side the circle of relatives of Fabaceae, which includes lentils, peas, and beans. It is easy to store seeds of greens from dry-seeded plant life. However, in case you want to keep seeds of vegetation which might be wet-seeded, then it'd eat an entire lot of time. We have said below in element the stairs for saving seeds. They will assist facilitate the approach of seed saving.

4.2.1 First Step: You must pick out and pick out up seed-saving substances

You can speedy acquire commonplace home devices as seed-saving materials. Nothing complicated is crucial. In order in order to accumulate seeds as fast as you find out they have got matured, it is a splendid concept to preserve a modest seed-saving bundle deal to be had. The following are the gadgets you can want:

A small pair of scissors or a pocketknife

Marker or a pen

Paper bags or envelopes.

Buckets or bowls made from plastic or metal

The Mason jars

four.2.2 Second step: Wait till the adulthood of the seeds

Seed harvesting is simple and amusing. Knowing whilst the seeds turn out to be mature further to ready for harvest is a ability. To acquire and hone this abilties, you can need to paintings with endurance. Therefore, do not be scared to discover and offer new topics a shot.

How do you discover that the dry-seeded vegetation are ready for harvest?

These signs and signs and symptoms will help making a decision the adulthood of dry seeds similarly to their readiness for harvest movement.

Seed pod or seed's colour

Depending on the plant, seed pods and mature seeds lose their green color but as an alternative will collect colorings that might be black, yellow, brown or beige. When the flowers are starting to fade, flowering vegetation should acquire right interest. The heads of seeds grow to be organized for harvesting once they flip brown.

Seed pod or seed's dryness

When they may be sufficiently dried, they reap their maturity level. Seed pods may be rolled in the fingers to check their dryness degree. To test for dryness, a few seeds, like spinach or onion, can be sliced open. They are mature on the identical time because the interior is starchy in preference to milky.

See if the seed pod or seed may be indifferent.

Maturity may be determined with the useful resource of the manner you're capable of detach the seed pod or seed. Some plants, like swiss chard, cilantro, and beet, are outcomes examined thru vigorously rubbing the stem. The falling of seeds confirms the adulthood of seeds. You can harvest dry seeds preceding to their attainment of maturity level if inclement weather is anticipated; their improvement will now not prevent even after they'll be eliminated from the plant. It is right for high-quality positive kinds.

How do you discover that the vegetation which is probably moist-seeded are organized for harvest?

Wet seeds can be hard to decide while they may be mature because it varies from crop to crop. Researching the splendid strategies to hold seeds from unique species is beneficial. You want to bear in mind that you want to wait for a first rate term previous to harvesting wet-seeded stop end result and greens. Even after they gain a diploma wherein they turn out to be secure to devour, the seeds will keep growing in size and excellent. For instance, you need to wait to pluck cucumbers and brinjals. You need to look at for the quantity when they turn out to be really ripe. Fruit have to be stored complete if it needs to be harvested early to stave off harm or ailment, and the seeds need to be left to ripen in advance than being eliminated.

## Chapter 5: Storage And Germination

You want to have perfect know-how and understanding of the subsequent in case you are interested in saving and storing seeds.

Proper garage techniques

Seed Germination, germination expenses and times

five.1 Proper storage strategies

Many seeds lose half of of in their viability in six months while stored in sizeable room conditions. Seeds with thicker seed coats often stay shorter lives than humans with more difficult seed coats. Storage temperature, collectively with seed moisture, must be stored low and under control for better storage.

Easy-to-study seed garage techniques

Listed below are the strategies for storing seeds properly and successfully.

Ensure that you are simplest storing nicely-dried seeds. They ought to be mature, new and healthful seeds.

Keeping them in a dry and funky region will growth the seeds' viability.

Moisture is with out trouble absorbed with the beneficial resource of seeds. Air-tight containers want for use to maintain dryness. You can use glass jars or tin cans for storing seeds. They want to have tight-becoming lids.

Utilization of material that can absorb moisture is strongly recommended. Effective moisture-soaking up gadgets consist of powdered milk, dry charcoal, dry wood ash, cooled rice, or small quantities of newspaper.

A sector vicinity of the sector have to be taken up for the drying material.

The bins must be labeled with the form of seed, place, and date of collection.

If the least bit feasible, factor out the seeds' preliminary viability percent. To try this, sow some seeds and depend range how a variety of them germinate correctly. For instance, if 8 out of 10 seeds germinate, the viability price is 80%. You can use this statistics to decide how a whole lot every sort of seed loses viability amongst harvest and planting.

Prevent fungus and bugs from negative seeds. Before putting in packing containers, integrate with dry ash, black pepper seed powder, or neem leaves. Alternatively, use cotton, castor bean, peanut, or neem extract: 1 tsp. Oil for 1 kg of seeds. Alternately, use naphthalene balls (1 or 2) regular with 10 kg of seed.

Keep out of reach of birds and rodents within the direction of storage.

five.2 Critical elements to don't forget

Once the seed has thoroughly dried, keep it in steel cans, glass jars, plastic baggage, or other bins with sealable lids.

Points to don't forget for sealed boxes

Moist seeds need to in no way be saved.

Only airtight bins have to be used.

Ensure the smooth country of the container.

Seed containers want to handiest be opened even as required.

# Chapter 6: Specific Crops Seed Saving Guides

Vegetable seeds from the lawn harvest may be saved. These seeds may be planted the following three hundred and sixty five days. In order to save seeds, a plant want to be selected, its seeds should be harvested at the right time, and its seeds ought to be carefully saved for the winter. Beans, peas, tomatoes, and peppers are all suitable flora for seed saving. They have seeds that need little to no precise coaching earlier than garage. Moreover, they've got self-pollinating flowers. Since biennial vegetation require developing seasons to set seeds, it is greater hard to save the seeds from biennial flora like carrots or beets. Cross-pollination is viable in plant life having separate male and girl plant life, collectively with maize and vine plants. The seed stress have to be saved natural, it actually is hard. Cross-pollination won't have an impact at the best of the contemporary-day-day harvest, but the seeds from this sort of pass will produce fruit that is one-of-a-type from that of the parent plant and will develop into vines. This frequently has negative outcomes on flavor and different traits. Heirlooms, conventional kinds, and open-pollinated flora are the fine for saving seeds for the reason that flora from the seeds typically resemble their dad and mom. Hybrid seeds saved from 3 hundred and sixty 5 days will probable now not produce the right equal plants the following 12 months. Hybrids, but, might be interesting to increase from saved seeds if you want to test in addition to see what you get.

6.1 Saving Vegetable Seeds

Seeds of greens which encompass lettuce, tomatoes, peppers, peas, cucumber, and beans, cucumbers may be effortlessly stored. The above-cited vegetable seeds self-pollinate. Moreover, they want less renovation close to the storing manner.

Learn to store the seeds of a bean.

When the bean flowers' pods are dried, starting to forehead and open, it's time to achieve the seeds. Take the dried pods off your vegetation, and earlier than shelling them, permit the seeds dry on waxed paper for two weeks. Shelled seeds ought to be saved in an hermetic box until planting time.

Learn saving seeds of cucumber.

When the plant's fruit is ripe, cucumber seeds want to be saved. Set apart a few cucumbers on the same time as you are deciding on them so that you can harvest the seeds later. Put the pulp and seeds in a area after removing them from the plant. After that, fill the field with definitely sufficient water to cover the seeds and pulp. Make sure to stir the aggregate now and again as it ferments for two to four days at room temperature. The useless seeds will float to the top after some days. Pour off the pulp as quickly because the best seeds have sunk to the lowest. Seeds should be washed with water before being positioned on wax paper. Leave for every week to dry. Until you are organized to plant, keep dry seeds in an hermetic area.

Learn to preserve the seeds of peas.

When peas are dry, turning brown, and the pods are starting to interrupt up open, much like with beans, it's time to start accumulating the seeds. Remove pods and permit them to dry for two weeks in advance than shelling, just like with beans. Till you are organized to plant, preserve the shelled seeds in an airtight discipline.

Learn saving seeds of the pepper.

When the fruit is absolutely ripe, gather the pepper seeds; the majority of the sorts will flip pink and start to shrivel. At that aspect, take the seeds out of the fruit in addition to permit them to dry for 2 to four days on wax paper. Then, till you are prepared to plant, preserve dry seeds in an hermetic subject.

Learn saving seeds of onion.

The flavor of an onion picked right from the lawn is really outstanding. However, there are some assets you need to be aware of in advance than you harvest onion seeds. There is a resurgence in interest in domestic gardening for reasons which can embody a desire for organically grown food, economic problems, or surely the pride of serving food which you cultivated your self. People are using the internet to discover about seed protection and to discover the richness and flavor of antique kinds. Your involvement within the method can be as easy as collecting onion seeds for future planting. We want to say a few words approximately the forms of onions from which you may harvest onion seeds earlier than we communicate the way to do it. Many of the seeds or devices bought from most important seed manufacturers are hybrids, meaning they had been produced with the aid of crossing figure types decided on for splendid trends. We get the quality of each kinds when they are combined. That's splendid, but there can be a capture if you want to achieve onion seed from the ones hybrids. If the preserved seeds ever germinate, they'll most possibly produce onions that have the developments of each one figure or the alternative, but no longer every. Therefore, the number one rule is to avoid accumulating onion seeds from hybrids. The subsequent element you have to be privy to is that onions are biennial. Only of their 2d year do biennials bloom and produce seeds. When the umbrels or flowering heads start to show brown, it's time to reap onion seeds. Place the stalks in a paper bag after carefully reducing them off a few inches underneath the top. For many weeks, hold the bag in a fab, dry location. Shake the heads vigorously in the bag to release the seeds once they're completely dry.

Learn saving seeds of a tomato.

When the tomato fruit is ripe, store the seeds. You can either set apart some tomatoes actually for the reason of saving seeds or squeeze a number of the pulp and seeds. Put the pulp and seeds in a field, then cover it with water. Allow the pulp to ferment at room temperature for 2 to four days whilst stirring on occasion. The useless seeds will waft to the top after some days. Pour off the pulp once the best seeds have sunk to the bottom. Place seeds on wax paper after giving them a water rinse. After in step with week of drying, preserve in an airtight discipline until planting time.

Learn saving seeds of okra.

The vegetable okra, regularly known as women' fingers, grows extended, thin, stable to consume pods inside the warmth season. If you plant okra on your garden, saving the seeds is an less expensive and smooth manner to get seeds for the subsequent one year. Okra plant life should be grown in soil that gets complete sun. Okra want to be planted in the spring in spite of the whole thing threat of frost has handed. Okra may additionally moreover moreover expand with little moisture. However, weekly watering will bring about greater okra seed pods. Make high-quality the plant life are separated from exceptional okra sorts if you need to preserve the seeds of an okra species from your garden. On the alternative, your seeds can be hybrid. Insects act as pollinators for okra. The okra seed pods would possibly probably have seeds which is probably a hybrid of the 2 species if an insect pollinates your plant life with pollen from a certainly one of a type type of okra. By cultivating only one shape of okra in your lawn, you could keep away from this. Whether you're cultivating okra seed pods for intake or amassing okra seeds will determine while to benefit okra seeds. A few months after planting, an okra plant vegetation and then produces seed pods. Harvesting time for seed pods grown for intake with the useful resource of people is when they will be round 3 inches (8 cm) lengthy. Okra seed collectors need to, but, wait a bit longer and permit the okra seed pod broaden as an entire lot as it can. The okra seed pods want to dry at the plant and begin to interrupt up or crack earlier than they may be picked. The pods can then be taken out and break up or twisted. Keep a bowl nearby because of the reality the seeds will fall out effortlessly. The seeds do no longer need to be washed because of the truth no fleshy vegetable rely clings to them. Instead, allow the seeds dry in reality for a few days before placing them in a refrigerator-steady discipline with a high-quality lid.

Learn saving seeds of turnip.

Turnips thrive in slight regions with cold nights. With numerous sorts supplying both the turnip root vegetable and in shape to be eaten veggies, they make a great addition in your very very own vegetable lawn. A few of your turnip plant life will be saved as seed vegetation in region of harvesting them for his or her greens due to the fact turnips are easy to grow from seed. To get the sweetest greens and turnips, plant the seeds inside the early spring or fall. Give your seedlings time to amplify until the vegetation wither and seed pods seem. Until they turn brown, keep an eye fixed fixed on the seed pods on a everyday basis. Apply pruning shears or a knife to the stems to reduce the seed pods off. Begin with the pods at the lowest of the plants due to the truth they generally emerge as ripe early. Seeds from green pods might not develop, so leave them at the plant until the whole pod turns brown. Press down to softly crack open the seed pods after placing them in a paper bag or among pieces of paper towel. Separate the final pod fragments of seeds. Put the seeds in a paper bag to permit the moisture out. On the outside of the envelope, write the kind of seed and the harvest one year. The envelope ought to be saved in a dry, cool area this is unfastened from pests or rodents that could eat the seeds.

## 6.2 Saving Fruit Seeds

Listed under is the manual for saving seeds of watermelon, melon, citrus, apples and berries.

Learn saving seeds of watermelon and melon.

Whenever the fruit will become mature, accumulate the seeds. Make fine to increase seed-generating varieties of watermelons in location of seedless watermelons in case you want to shop seeds to plant the subsequent 12 months. After putting off the fruit's seeds, rinse them in a strainer to dispose of all the pulp. The seeds should then be spread out on wax paper to dry for approximately in keeping with week. Until they may be certainly dry, turn them as speedy as each day. Until you're prepared to plant, store dry seeds in an hermetic container.

Learn saving seeds of citrus.

Starting with a piece seed and searching it turn out to be a complete-fledged plant is interesting. It is essential to maintain in mind that, within the case of citrus tree seeds, the seed you plant from, allow's take into account, a Valencia orange, won't have the same abilities because the original orange tree. This is so because of the fact fruit timber used for trade are made from extremely good factors. Stock, or rootstock, makes up the lower trunk and root device. The tissue of the chosen citrus is inserted into the rootstock to create the scion. This allows the economic citrus manufacturer to adjust the fruit's tendencies and choose out only the ones functions that make the fruit the maximum marketable and applicable. Citrus seeds can be with out issue amassed. Get the diverse cease result you need to develop. By doing this, the possibility of having seedlings is extended. Seeds need to be pressed lightly. Ensure that they'll be no longer broken within the route of the approach. Remove the sugar this is stuck to the seeds by means of using rinsing them in water; sugar fosters fungal increase and endangers viable seedlings. Put them on a bit of paper. Sort the maximum vital seeds; the maximum feasible ones might be greater white than tan with a contracted outer skin. The seeds can now be planted or prepared for citrus seed garage. Citrus seeds need to be positioned on a wet paper towel for garage features. In case some of the seeds are not possible, maintain 3 instances as many as you want to plant. In a plastic bag that can be sealed, wrap the seeds in a paper towel. Put the bag inside the refrigerator. Citrus seeds can be saved inside the fridge for some days to numerous months. Citrus seeds, now not like extraordinary seeds, require constant moisture. They are pretty probable no longer to germinate within the event that they dry out.

# Chapter 7: Planning A Seed Garden

If you need to preserve seeds for your lawn, you then ought to begin with a plan because it will make your task tons less complicated and help you get viable seeds that produce actual-to-kind flora.

You have to determine the vegetation that you want to plant. You need to have the functionality and professional to make most use of your region. You need to make certain that every crop is planted at the right time. You can expand a garden through doing little planning. You can in the long run harvest the vegetables and quit end result and accumulate exquisite seeds. Listed below are the pointers to help you get began out out:

7.1 Know what species you are planting.

You can determine which of your vegetation may go-pollinate thru using facts the medical call of the species of flora you are planting. Then you may take movement to prevent it.

7.2 Plant Selection and Seed Quality

To maintain the super seed, we need to start with the high-quality flowers. You must select and purchase seeds whose wonderful is proper. You should make your lawn a success via adhering to this precept. Quality seeds will continuously offer you with incredible effects and convey. The skills of seeds want to be registered. These capabilities consist of plant power and germination. Moreover, you want to furthermore be aware about their vulnerability to disease and bugs. The data as a end result received is beneficial in locating out the seeds which might be awesome, and that may be planted inside the garden.

7.Three Know at the same time as your vegetation will seed

Biennial plant life, like onions and carrots, do no longer flower till their 2nd growing season, which comes after wintry climate. Annual flowers flower, produce seed and die in a single developing season. Asparagus and fruit wood are examples of prolonged-lasting perennials that flower again and again for decades. Planning for seed saving is made less difficult whilst you understand whilst to anticipate seeds.

7.Four Get sufficient sun

Most flora want whole solar to deliver seeds whose exquisite is immoderate. Plants are powered through the usage of manner of sun electricity, so once they gather plenty of daylight hours, they mature greater rapid and are more potent. Since leafy flowers collectively with lettuce and spinach can bear much less sunshine, gardeners often develop them in shade or detail color on the town gardens wherein it might be tough to find sunny spots some of the wood and homes. Because generating fruit and seeds calls for introduced electricity than generating leaves, many plant life can stay to tell the story in shaded areas without blooming. Remember which you for the time being are growing seeds if this is your plan for developing veggies. If you only need the leaves, then lettuce, spinach, and other leafy greens are properly in partial colour, however they require greater solar power to provide plants and seeds.

7.5 Keep it easy

Use self-pollinating plant life or plant best one variant of every species in case you're a newbie to avoid getting pass-pollinated seeds.

7.6 Prevent pass-pollination via setting apart kinds.

You ought to maintain your seeds from getting cross-pollinated with different sorts if you want them to broaden "right to type" or just like the plants they got here from. To prevent plants from crossing, discover which ones do (pumpkins and zucchini do, but now not watermelons) and the manner a long way aside they must be planted. Additionally, recollect the gardens of your buddies and how far away they'll be from yours. You may probable want to develop multiple plant type from the same species because of the truth many delectable greens are circulate-pollinators. Fortunately, you may avoid pass-pollination with the resource of way of taking a few steps.

Isolate the flowers properly.

Maintain an great sufficient distance among your flowers to prevent bypass-pollination. Plants that flow-pollinate require area this is adequate, called the isolation distance. The motive of this approach is to offer seeds which might be real to the determine plant. Every specie calls for particular isolation distances.

Planting instances need to be staggered.

A minimal duration of 14 days is essential to skip among plantings of various sorts to save you flowering times from overlapping. For this to artwork, you need to be aware of the time each kind requires to mature.

Physical limitations need to be used.

One variety can be blanketed at a time using a bodily barrier. You can use a row cover or blossom bag for this purpose. Don't forget about to offer each type sufficient publicity time that permits you to pollinate each other.

Plants need to be pollinated with the help of palms

In order to prevent the plants from flow-pollination, there are some of hand-pollination strategies that can be used. When you pollinate with the useful resource of the usage of your fingers, you manually switch the male flora' pollen to the woman flora.

Adhere to crop rotation precept.

Crop rotation is the workout of growing particular vegetable classes in certainly one of a kind areas of the vegetable plot each one year. This organizes groupings of flowers steady with their cultivation necessities and aids in the discount of pest and sickness issues which might be precise to a given crop. There are severa annual plants that can be grown anywhere, together with candy corn, endive, lettuce, cucumbers, marrows, pumpkins, squashes, and courgettes. They shouldn't be grown within the same location. Before the developing season begins offevolved, plan your crop rotation and mark the ground with plot markers so you will understand wherein to place every crop. Crop rotation increases soil fertility, enhances weed manage techniques, and aids in pest and ailment control.

7.Eight Ensure there can be greater location.

You accumulate the seeds of tomatoes and pumpkins on the same time as they may be mature. But you need to bear in mind that it is going to take more time for greens which might be biennial, radishes, broccoli, zucchini, lettuce, and cucumber. Additionally, whilst plants produce plants and seeds, they may broaden in top and/or width. For example, head lettuces may be grown without problem with a distance of one foot; but, as they reap their whole seed-bearing length, you'll want to go away not much less than 1 ½ ft. You can plant them at a distance which you use normally. More place need to really take delivery of to the others in order that the seeds can achieve their adulthood. Lettuce seeds can be planted indoors. This permits their germination, especially at the equal time as there is no humidity in summer season, relying on the range and your weather.

7.Nine Seeds ought to be gathered in baggage.

Seeds can be collected without issue on the same time as you vicinity paper luggage of small size atop the seed pods or seed heads.

7.10 Ensure entire dryness of seeds.

Test the dryness of your seeds by using manner of the use of pushing the nail of a finger into one of the elements. Formation of dent approach that they may be now not dry enough. They are prepared for storage if there aren't any dents.

7.11 Oven have to now not be used for drying seeds.

Whatever may be the environment, be it humid or dry, an oven ought to now not be used for drying seeds. Seeds may be broken if the seeds collect a totally high temperature.

## Chapter 8: Edible And Nutritious Seeds

Some wholesome for human intake seeds not only taste first rate but also are a terrific deliver of severa nutrients and vitamins. Many human beings overlook the truth that some seeds may be eaten and pleasant view seeds as subjects to plant at the manner to make bigger different things. Although they may now not appear to be doing an lousy lot inside the smoothie or salad bowl, seeds are actually nutritious. Many incorporate fiber and omega-3 to manual the coronary coronary coronary heart and assist your digestive system paintings nicely. Furthermore, seeds are a superb supply of protein, making them a smooth way to enhance your strength tiers, especially if you're a vegetarian or vegan who desires meat options. They are top notch for hiking because of the fact they may be available to keep as a snack. Now we will speak some safe to consume seeds that you could upload in your weight loss plan.

eight.1 Chia Seeds

The Aztecs ate severa chia seeds because of the truth they originated from Mexico. They are small, black and white Salvia hispanica plant seeds. They're a top notch supply of calcium, phosphorus, magnesium, and omega-3 fatty acids. Chia seeds have been fantastically well-known over the past ten years because of their huge fitness advantages. Chia seeds can be carried out in yogurt and oatmeal , similarly to smoothies. By combining them with milk and refrigerating them in a unmarried day, you could additionally use them to make chia pudding. Chia seeds are a fantastic manner to feature texture in your food even as obtaining fitness blessings.

## 8.2 Sesame seeds

Sesame seeds are small, brown or black seeds with a nutty taste that are produced through manner of the Sesamum indicum plant. Although sesame seeds are maximum normally associated with hamburger buns, they may be a commonplace detail in lots of different cuisines all around the world. They're a common element in Asian cooking, as an instance, and are utilized in dishes like sushi, stir-fries, and grilled meats. If you want to boom the quantity of magnesium, copper, calcium, iron, and zinc on your food regimen, sesame seeds are a fantastic choice. They moreover consist of phytosterols, which is probably substances that may aid in reducing levels of cholesterol. Sesame seeds may be sprinkled on top of salads or added to stir-fries. They can also be used for making tahini, a sesame seed paste famous in Middle Eastern cooking.

8. Three Pumpkin seeds

The Cucurbita maxima plant produces pepitas, which can be every other call for pumpkin seeds. They are small, inexperienced seeds with a nutty taste. There is a lot of magnesium, zinc, and iron in pumpkin seeds. They are beneficial in case you need to growth the amount of fiber in your diet plan. Raw pumpkin seeds have a moderate taste. They are, consequently, a surely best and on hand snack for any time of the day. Pumpkin seeds flavor remarkable in cereal and green smoothies, but you can eat them on their personal to experience their chewy consistency. For a unique flavor, you can additionally strive incorporating them into pesto or guacamole.

## Chapter 9: Troubleshooting And Faqs

First, we're in a position to speak about a way to perceive and cope with special issues associated with seeds.

nine.1 Troubleshooting and answers to capability issues

Although we're hoping that your sowing plan is extraordinary and powerful, we've got were given compiled a listing of recommendations for identifying and resolving troubles with germination in addition to more youthful seedlings.

How to cope with germination problems?

There isn't always any want to fear if there are not any seedlings. Fresh food has a shelf existence. This is likewise real for seeds. If doubtful, check the seed packs and do a short check of germination to make certain whether or now not or now not the seeds can be sown. If they can't be sown, then they should be discarded. While the seeds of certain vegetables, together with parsnip together with onion, best closing a 12 months, those of others can be stored successfully for a most of five years. The viability of a seed is likewise notably inspired through how it is saved.

How can timing be ensured?

Sometimes seedlings do no longer appear without a doubt because of the reality they couldn't get the time required for germination. Verify the ordinary germination times listed on seed packets, however keep in mind that they observe in most suitable times.

What can we do to preserve the appropriate temperature?

Various seeds require numerous temperatures. Warm-season greens determine upon temperatures above 20°C (68°F). To ensure seeds are cosseted well, are trying to find recommendation from seed packs and join up the soil degree temperature. Heat mats facilitate in developing the temperature and keeping it, whilst a coloration cloth need to useful useful resource in fending off warmness climate.

How to avoid moisture?

Wet seeds can rot previous to germination, whilst seeds which is probably too dry won't get the sign to sprout. Take a twig bottle and spray the seed sowing mixture previous to filling it in bins.

How are we able to remove Damping Off?

Your seedlings begin to increase, however as quickly as they do, they fall over and wither. 'Damping off' is the motive of this commonplace problem. The answer is to continually make sure there can be superb air glide on the identical time as being careful now not to overwater. Use smooth pots, trays, and seed-starting combination always. Water seedlings with sparkling mains water instead of rainfall that has been status round.

How do I solve the trouble of moldy potting soil?

Though it is dubious that inexperienced or white mildew on the soil's ground will surely harm seedlings, it's miles an illustration that the basis location is overly damp. Take it as a warning and take appropriate movement. To increase air waft round seedlings, begin thru way of carefully scraping off the mildew. Then, if critical, open all of the greenhouse's vents. When you water seedlings from below, the hazard of ground mildew development is reduced.

How can we dispose of Fungus Gnats?

Fungus gnats are maximum probable the marginally perceptible flies darting about simply above the soil line. While individual flies can not damage plant life, their larvae can do so with the aid of manner of the usage of feeding at the roots and stopping seedlings from growing. You have a few alternatives if you stumble upon fungus gnats. You must provide seedlings a chunk time to dry out amongst waterings.

What can we do to avoid leggy seedlings?

Poor mild tiers are typically indicated by means of using stretched seedlings with wide areas among gadgets of leaves and a frequently mild complexion. They may also be signs and signs and signs and symptoms of crowding or an excessive amount of warm temperature. These reasons may be handled surely. Move seedlings to a brighter windowsill or recollect installing develop lighting fixtures early inside the developing season to alleviate a lack of mild, that is often determined with the resource of seedlings leaning within the path of a moderate supply.

## 9.2 Common Challenges in Seed Saving

One element that made seed saving extra difficult for farmers and breeders was the 1970 Plant Variety Protection Act, which protects the intellectual assets rights of plant breeders. Small farmers regularly lack the assets to store seeds or rent patented seeds to create new sorts. Over 50% of all seed income are underneath the palms of four seed firms. With a whole lot lots less seed availability, variety, and version because of market interest, growers are furnished with seeds that don't have any ancient cost. In order to create a hybrid, genetically separate plant populations ought to interbreed. It is volatile to save seeds from hybridized vegetation due to the truth they might not develop the equal plant the subsequent three hundred and sixty five days, and in lots of situations, they will not produce any flowers the least bit. Growers can save coins with the aid of no longer having to buy seeds every yr, which takes cash a long way from large agencies. Saving seeds can bring about monetary economic economic financial savings with a few essential devices and little try. Local growers can reap seeds at a lesser price than large retail companies way to resources like seed swaps, a place in which manufacturers can exchange seeds, and seed libraries, wherein people can borrow seeds at the start of the growing season and pass returned saved seeds at the give up of the season. Saving seeds can help ensure seed availability and lessen farms' dependency on large businesses and erratic deliver networks. It lets in you to develop what you want, now not counting on a company to offer food for you and your community, and having the freedom to choose what flourishes in this environment. It gives you pleasure to stay related in this manner. Amazing flavor and resilience are produced through using the interaction of soil, climate, and animals. Saving seeds offers every ecological and economic benefits, particularly in slight of weather change. Heirloom seeds, as an instance, have a wealthy genetic historical past that makes them able to respond to environmental changes. If you can assemble a hospitable enough surroundings, deciding on resiliency furthermore way choosing self-sufficiency, as you might not need to depend on companies or outdoor assets on your meals. Smaller corporations in some distance flung areas use the maximum commonplace strategies of seed storage. Although they may be not regularly taken beneath interest, conventional seed maintenance strategies offer essential insights into the way to beautify current strategies. Inadequate garage techniques had been found to growth moisture absorption, which favors the increase of pests and illnesses, insect infestation, alongside facet fungal infection, ultimately degrading the amazing and viability of seeds. According to study effects, special storage kinds supply a special degree of danger for those problems. The need to accumulate species-specific know-how is some unique undertaking with lengthy-time period seed garage. In big facilities, seeds are presently cryogenically maintained with out distinction. Lack of knowledge, patenting and highbrow rights have additionally made it very difficult to keep proper kinds of seeds for better produce.

9.Three You can keep seeds regardless of the growing disturbing conditions.

Anybody can take pleasure in seed-saving sports activities activities. In order to have plant life which may be greater applicable to their surroundings the following year, gardeners want to choose out plant life having incredible first rate. They need to moreover be sturdy sufficient to deliver seeds. To keep away from drift-pollination inside the beginning, it have to be decided via gardeners whether or not the flowers they need to provide are open-pollinated or hybrid. They have to have a easy records of plant life' pollination manner. The distance desired among flowers to keep away from cross-pollination is called the isolation distance. Growers need to select out healthful vegetation at the same time as deciding on seeds. To maintain matters clean, beginners may also start with flowers like tomatoes, peppers, and beans that generate seeds in their planting season. It is notable for growers that the seed ought to be harvested after its maturity. You need to keep and keep seeds in a place this is dry and cool; refrigerators artwork high-quality for this. Farmers can rely lots much less on others, be aware of the fitness in their plants, and be associated with their surroundings thru saving seeds. Owning your personal seeds, developing them, and choosing the functions you price, might be a delivery of delight and a experience of empowerment.

## Chapter 10: The Magic Of Seed Conservation

Seeds are the tiny pills of existence that maintains internal them the capacity for a future complete of lush, green landscapes and bountiful harvests. The act of seed conservation isn't always something quick of magical, because it ensures the preservation of genetic range and the continuation of existence on Earth.

Time Travel: A Brief History and Culture behind Seed Conservation

In the problematic tapestry of our worldwide records and way of existence, the practice of seed conservation stands as a testament to humanity's functionality to traverse time. This top notch employer, rooted in historic traditions and constantly evolving, allows us to protect the past and destiny of our planet's biodiversity. Seed conservation is not most effective an critical tool for ensuring food safety however additionally a journey thru time, connecting us with our agricultural historical past and keeping the genetic richness of our plant species.

Ancient Beginnings

The exercise of seed saving has ancient origins, courting decrease decrease lower back hundreds of years to the earliest human agricultural endeavors. In ancient civilizations along with Mesopotamia, China, and the Indus Valley, farmers intuitively identified the rate of gathering and replanting seeds from their high-quality plant life. This rudimentary shape of seed conservation laid the basis for the destiny of agriculture.

Cultural Significance

Over time, the exercise of seed saving superior proper into a cultural tradition deeply intertwined with the identities of numerous companies spherical the area. For Indigenous peoples, seed saving is an critical a part of their cultural records. The Native American Three Sisters planting technique, for instance, showcases the synergy amongst corn, beans, and squash, demonstrating no longer best agricultural information but moreover a profound data of biodiversity and sustainable agriculture.

Similarly, in Asia, rice types had been handed down through generations. The fragrant Basmati rice, for instance, has been cultivated in the Indian subcontinent for loads of years and is widely known for its specific taste and fragrance. The renovation of such traditional rice types now not only keeps cultural identity but moreover guarantees agricultural resilience and meals safety.

In Europe, seed saving modified into additionally crucial to agrarian societies. Heirloom styles of greens like tomatoes, cucumbers, and pumpkins had been cherished for their flavor and specific attributes, and the workout of saving seeds have become a manner for households to skip down their agricultural ancient past.

The Green Revolution and the Decline of Diversity

The mid-20th century brought about large modifications in agricultural practices with the appearance of the Green Revolution. This generation have become marked via the significant adoption of high-yielding crop kinds, often on the cost of conventional and locally tailor-made seeds. While the ones new sorts multiplied food production, in addition they triggered a decline in agricultural variety as conventional and heirloom types have been changed.

The cognizance on a confined massive shape of high-yielding flora contributed to the dearth of many indigenous and locally adapted plant kinds. As a quit end result, agricultural biodiversity became threatened, and the cultural significance of many conventional seed-saving practices started out to wane.

The Modern Seed Conservation Movement

Recognizing the want to hold biodiversity and the cultural significance of seed saving, the current seed conservation movement emerged. Organizations and seed banks, which includes the Svalbard Global Seed Vault in Norway and the Millennium Seed Bank in the United Kingdom, were hooked up to accumulate, catalog, and defend seeds from round the area.

These projects intention to make certain that the genetic variety of plant species is blanketed for destiny generations. In the face of climate change, rising plant ailments, and the want for added sustainable agriculture, maintaining a large range of plant genetics is vital for food protection and agricultural resilience.

Community Seed Banks and Reviving Traditions

While large-scale seed banks play a essential role in seed conservation, community-primarily based totally efforts are similarly crucial. Community seed banks, regularly run thru network companies and farmers, attention on maintaining close by and heirloom sorts. These banks engage organizations in seed saving, sharing know-how, and celebrating the cultural importance of conventional seeds.

Furthermore, the idea of open-source seed sharing has received momentum in modern years. Seed libraries and exchange networks allow humans to percentage seeds freely, promoting the idea that seeds are a commonplace ancient beyond. This motion fosters a experience of community and encourages the revival of seed-saving traditions, connecting human beings to their agricultural roots.

The Global Seed Vault

The Svalbard Global Seed Vault, frequently called the "Doomsday Vault," stands as an iconic photograph of the place's commitment to retaining agricultural biodiversity. Located deep within the Arctic permafrost, this solid facility houses over a million seed samples from across the globe. It serves as a worldwide backup device, protecting the genetic type of our most essential plant life.

The Global Seed Vault is a beacon of desire for humanity, imparting a shield in opposition to unforeseen catastrophes, be they natural or guy-made. It demonstrates our collective responsibility to ensure the legacy of seed conservation maintains, allowing future generations to enjoy the genetic assets which have sustained life on our planet for millennia.

Seed Conservation within the Face of Climate Change

Climate alternate poses a massive project to seed conservation efforts. With growing temperatures and increasingly unpredictable weather patterns, the adaptability of plant species will become of most significance. Seeds that have been conserved through the years can function a reservoir of genetic inclinations, allowing us to reproduce new crop types that would withstand changing environmental situations.

In the face of climate change, seed conservation takes on even extra significance.

As we witness the displacement of agricultural zones and shifts in growing seasons, get proper of get right of entry to to to a severa shape of seeds with particular trends turns into vital for ensuring meals safety and resilience within the agricultural location.

The Green Legacy: Environmental, Economic Benefits, and Beyond

The exercise of seed conservation, regularly hailed because the inexperienced legacy of our planet, holds massive importance far past maintaining biodiversity. This project gives severa blessings, which includes environmental sustainability, meals safety, financial stability, and cultural maintenance, fostering a more resilient, sustainable, and interconnected global society.

1. Environmental Resilience and Biodiversity Preservation

The center of seed conservation lies in environmental resilience and retaining biodiversity. It safeguards the genetic belongings of severa plant species, making sure adaptability to changing environmental situations, countering pests, illnesses, and climate change. This genetic variety enables the balance and fitness of ecosystems, reaping benefits each flowers and fauna.

2. Sustainable Agriculture and Food Security

Seed conservation is pivotal for sustainable agriculture and international food safety. Preserving severa seed sorts allows agricultural resilience, reducing dependence on chemical substances and enhancing sustainability. In the face of a growing international population and weather exchange demanding situations, it offers a protection internet toward crop screw ups, ensuring a robust food supply, specifically in risky areas.

3. Economic Stability and Agricultural Innovation

Seed conservation contributes to economic stability and agricultural innovation. It encourages the improvement of latest crop types with higher yields, improved nutrients, and pest resistance. This boosts productivity and creates monetary possibilities whilst keeping cultural heritage and assisting close by economies.

4. Scientific Advancements and Global Collaboration

The inexperienced legacy of seed conservation fuels scientific improvements and international collaboration. Seed banks and initiatives facilitate sharing genetic assets, using progressive agricultural solutions and promoting global cooperation. This shared commitment fosters global group spirit and mutual obligation for our planet's natural resources.

5. Educational and Community Engagement

Seed conservation serves as an educational platform and encourages network engagement. It gives possibilities to discover about biodiversity, sustainable agriculture, and environmental stewardship, fostering an information of environment interconnectedness. Community involvement empowers humans to grow to be stewards of community biodiversity, selling social concord and sustainability.

Chapter 2:

Gardening 101 - Creating Your Green Oasis

Embarking on the journey to create your very very personal green oasis is an exciting enterprise that ensures a deep reference to nature and the pride of nurturing lifestyles. Whether you have a sprawling outside or a modest balcony, the standards of sustainable gardening may be executed to any place, huge or small.

The Blank Canvas: Choosing the Ideal Area for Your Sustainable Garden

Embarking on the adventure to create a sustainable lawn is an thrilling employer, but the first step is perhaps the maximum important: selecting the ideal place for your green oasis. The determined on place will set the degree for your lawn's success and its environmental impact. By thinking about key factors which embody daylight, soil remarkable, and get right of access to to water, you could redesign your clean canvas right into a flourishing and sustainable garden that advantages each the surroundings and your properly-being.

Sunlight

Sunlight is the artist's paintbrush in terms of gardening. It is the number one electricity deliver that fuels photosynthesis, allowing plants to convert daytime into meals. Therefore, the number one hobby in selecting a lawn area is daylight availability.

Assess Sunlight Patterns: Observe the types of sunlight for your capability lawn place. Most vegetables, flowers, and lots of herbs thrive with at the least 6-eight hours of direct daylight steady with day. Plants in conjunction with tomatoes, peppers, and sunflowers are considered "complete solar" and require sufficient slight to flourish. Shadier spots may be extra appropriate for vegetation like leafy veggies, first-class herbs, or shade-loving decorative species.

Microclimates: Be privy to microclimates inside your lawn area. Factors which incorporates houses, partitions, and bushes can create microclimates which have an impact on temperature and daylight. These microclimates can be first-rate if you goal to extend your growing season or offer colour for particular vegetation.

Soil Quality

The subsequent issue to bear in mind is the splendid of the soil in your preferred region. Soil is the inspiration upon which your garden will thrive, and its health is pivotal for sustainable gardening practices.

Conduct a Soil Test: Before planting, it is definitely useful to conduct a soil take a look at to evaluate its pH diploma, nutrient composition, and regular nice. You should buy soil trying out kits or speak with community agricultural extensions to benefit professional soil assessment. The consequences will manual you on any critical amendments, which include together with natural rely range to enhance soil form or adjusting pH tiers.

Drainage: Evaluate the soil's drainage functionality. Well-draining soil prevents waterlogged roots and decreases the threat of root rot. If your lawn place has awful drainage, endure in mind raised beds or incorporating natural rely to enhance soil aeration.

Water Source

Access to water is a important hassle of sustainable gardening. Water conservation isn't always handiest an environmental responsibility but moreover a practical consideration for retaining a thriving garden.

Proximity to Water: Choose a garden place this is near a water supply, in conjunction with a rain barrel, lawn hose, or irrigation tool. This will make watering greater available and green.

Consider Rainfall Patterns: Take underneath consideration your location's average rainfall patterns. If you stay in an area with common rainfall, you may need plenty much less irrigation, even as in drier climates, you may need to put money into water-efficient irrigation systems or drought-tolerant plant types.

Rainwater Harvesting: Embrace sustainable practices like rainwater harvesting. Collecting rainwater in barrels or cisterns can offer an green water supply for your lawn, decreasing the need for municipal water and retaining this treasured beneficial resource.

Accessibility and Convenience

The comfort and accessibility of your lawn area play a important position on your gardening revel in and sustainability efforts.

Proximity to the Home: Consider the proximity of your garden to your own home. A garden this is towards your dwelling vicinity is more likely to be frequently tended to and monitored for pests, illnesses, and watering goals.

Accessibility for Maintenance: Ensure that your lawn region is obtainable for safety obligations, along side weeding, harvesting, and soil amendments. Paths or walkways should make it simpler to navigate through the garden with out compacting the soil.

Safety and Visibility: Keep protection and visibility in mind, particularly when you have children or pets. Choose a lawn place that lets in for easy sightlines to supervise out of doors sports even as moreover considering potential protection dangers, together with poisonous vegetation.

Environmental Considerations

Sustainable gardening is, by using the usage of using its very nature, harmonious with the surroundings. When deciding on your lawn region, consider the manner it aligns with ecological standards.

Native Plant Integration: If feasible, undergo in thoughts incorporating close by plant species into your garden format. Native flora are properly-suitable to community situations, stressful a whole lot much less water and preservation, on the identical time as also supplying essential habitat and meals assets for neighborhood plant life and fauna.

Wildlife-Friendly Features: Create herbal global-high-quality competencies on your garden, consisting of fowl feeders, butterfly gardens, or small water functions. These factors beautify the ecological fee of your garden and inspire biodiversity.

Environmental Impact: Assess the potential environmental impact of your lawn region.

Avoid locations which could disrupt herbal habitats or contribute to soil erosion. Instead, purpose to decorate the encircling surroundings thru selecting sustainable planting alternatives.

Essential Tools to Begin

Starting a gardening adventure can be a profitable and enriching revel in. Whether you're trying to cultivate lovable flowers, develop your very personal food, or create a sustainable oasis, having the proper system is vital on your success. Here, we'll discover the important gadget each amateur gardener must take into account to get started out out on the right foot.

1. Hand Trowel

A hand trowel is one of the maximum versatile and important device for any gardener. This compact, handheld tool is right for obligations which include digging, transplanting, weeding, and making holes for small vegetation and bulbs. Look for a trowel with a cushty cope with and an extended lasting, rust-resistant blade to make your gardening duties greater inexperienced.

2. Pruners or Secateurs

Pruners, additionally called secateurs, are used for decreasing stems, branches, and lifeless increase to your vegetation. They are to be had in numerous styles, along with bypass pruners (which art work like scissors) and anvil pruners (that have a blade that cuts in the direction of a flat ground). Select a style that aligns along with your requirements and invest in a pinnacle-notable pair for precise, smooth cuts that decorate plant health.

three. Garden Gloves

Garden gloves are crucial for keeping your arms smooth and guarded while strolling inside the lawn. They protect your pores and pores and skin from dirt, thorns, and capacity irritants. Look for gloves that healthful nicely and provide accurate grip while taking into consideration dexterity to cope with diverse gardening duties.

4. Garden Fork

A garden fork is a treasured device for turning and loosening soil, breaking apart clumps, and incorporating compost or other soil amendments. It's vital for buying prepared your garden beds, improving soil aeration, and selling wholesome root growth.

five. Rake

A rake is vital for leveling soil, spreading mulch, removing leaves, and retaining your lawn tidy. Invest in a long lasting garden rake with adjustable tines, which permits you to evolve the tool to super garden duties.

6. Watering Can or Hose

Proper watering is essential for plant fitness, so having a reliable watering can or hose is a need to. A watering can is great for smaller gardens or potted plant life, on the identical time as a garden hose is suitable for big regions. Look for a hose with an adjustable nozzle for control over water go along with the float.

7. Wheelbarrow or Garden Cart

A wheelbarrow or garden cart is valuable for transporting soil, mulch, flora, and heavy gardening materials. It reduces strain to your decrease returned and makes responsibilities like transferring compost or mulch a exceptional deal greater ability.

8. Soil pH Tester

Understanding your soil's pH level is important for a achievement gardening. A soil pH tester, normally available as a handheld probe or meter, aids in assessing whether or not or not your soil is acidic, independent, or alkaline. Understanding your soil's pH lets in you to pick out flowers a brilliant way to flourish on your garden and make knowledgeable options about soil amendments.

9. Garden Pruner Sharpener

Keeping your pruners, shears, and special lowering device sharp is critical for smooth and wholesome cuts. A lawn pruner sharpener is a convenient device that guarantees your cutting machine stays in fine circumstance. Regular upkeep prolongs the lifespan of your system and helps save you damage in your plant life.

10. Garden Kneeler/Seat

Gardening may be physically traumatic, so a garden kneeler/seat offers comfort and assist. It's a flexible device that permits you to kneel or take a seat at the same time as gardening, lowering stress in your knees and decrease back. Some models even come with integrated wallet for wearing gear and substances.

eleven. Garden Shears or Hedge Trimmers

If you have got were given hedges or shrubs for your lawn, a superb pair of lawn shears or hedge trimmers is crucial for shaping and maintaining their appearance. They make pruning and trimming responsibilities extra inexperienced and help keep your panorama looking neat and properly-maintained.

12. Garden Weeder

Weeding is a vital chore in any lawn. A lawn weeder, regularly with a forked or hooked surrender, lets in you get rid of weeds from the soil with minimal disturbance to your selected flowers. Choose one which fits your specific weeding wishes, whether or not for huge lawn beds or tight areas.

thirteen. Garden Apron or Tool Belt

A lawn apron or tool belt is a accessible accessory that keeps your important device internal easy reach. It's mainly beneficial while you are moving round your lawn, planting, and appearing numerous responsibilities. Look for one with pockets and booths for storing trowels, pruners, and different small gear.

14. Garden Shovel

A garden shovel is critical for digging holes for planting, shifting soil, and transplanting large plant life. Look for a sturdy and well-balanced shovel with a cushty grip to make your digging obligations greater doable.

15. Garden Twine or String

Garden cord or string is a versatile device for staking plant life, developing trellises, and organizing your garden. It permits help hiking flowers, keep rows right away, and regular vegetation to save you wind harm.

Chapter three:

Choose with Heart - Discover and Select Your Green Gems

In the pursuit of a colourful and thriving garden, selecting the proper plant life is paramount. This phase will guide you thru the method of discovering and choosing green gem stones that now not first-class contribute to the beauty of your lawn however moreover play a essential function in seed conservation efforts. Additionally, we are able to delve into the crucial practices of figuring out wholesome plant life and spotting those that would pose risks for your garden's primary nicely-being.

Selecting Plants for Seed Conservation

Seed conservation is a vital exercising for retaining biodiversity, making sure food protection, and selling sustainable gardening. Selecting the proper flowers for seed conservation is a crucial step on this way. Whether you're inquisitive about saving seeds from food plant life, ornamental plants, or nearby species, know-how the standards and techniques for plant choice is important.

1. Genetic Diversity

Genetic range is the cornerstone of seed conservation. To pick plant life for conservation, it's miles vital to prioritize species or types that represent a large genetic pool. A severa gene pool enables vegetation adapt to changing environmental situations and withstand pests and ailments.

Choose Heirloom and Open-Pollinated Varieties: Heirloom vegetation and open-pollinated sorts are brilliant alternatives for seed conservation because of the reality they usually usually tend to hold genetic range. These vegetation have frequently been cultivated for generations, making them treasured reservoirs of genetic records.

Local and Indigenous Species: Native and indigenous plant species are tailor-made to close by climates and soil conditions. They regularly very own precise genetic dispositions that purpose them to precious for seed conservation. By prioritizing the ones species, you assist the protection of nearby biodiversity.

2. Plant Health and Vigor

Healthy, lively flora are much more likely to deliver exquisite seeds. When choosing flora for seed conservation, prioritize folks who show off sturdy boom, illness resistance, and pest tolerance. Here are some key problems:

Observation and Selection: Monitor the plants to your lawn or conservation vicinity in the course of the developing season. Select seeds from the healthiest and most complete of life people that showcase relevant traits.

Avoid Disease-Prone Plants: Plants which is probably commonly tormented by illnesses may also additionally pass on those vulnerabilities to their offspring. Be careful while saving seeds from flora with a statistics of disease problems.

three. Pollination Methods

Understanding the pollination strategies of the vegetation you need to hold is critical. Different pollination strategies impact how seeds are saved and maintained.

Self-Pollinated Plants: Self-pollinating plant life, which includes beans and tomatoes, are commonly simpler to shop seeds from. They have a better degree of genetic consistency for the cause that they normally fertilize themselves. To save you circulate-pollination, isolate self-pollinated flora from extraordinary types of the identical species.

Cross-Pollinated Plants: Cross-pollinated flowers, like cucumbers and corn, require more meticulous isolation strategies. To hold their genetic purity, you want to prevent cross-pollination with wonderful kinds of the identical species, frequently via physical barriers like distance or time separation.

four. Planting Space and Isolation

Maintaining genetic purity is vital for seed conservation. Cross-pollination among awesome sorts can result in hybrid seeds, compromising the integrity of the conserved range. Here's a way to save you bypass-pollination:

Spatial Isolation: Plant definitely considered one of a type styles of the same species at a fantastic distance aside. This bodily separation minimizes the opportunities of pass-pollination with the useful resource of wind, insects, or specific pollinators.

Time Isolation: Some flowers can be separated by using their flowering times to keep away from bypass-pollination. Planting early and overdue kinds of the equal species can assist prevent genetic blending.

Hand Pollination: For flora in which isolation isn't feasible, maintain in thoughts hand-pollination. This includes manually moving pollen from one flower to every different to control pollination and preserve genetic purity.

five. Disease Resistance and Tolerance

Selecting plants with a statistics of disease resistance or tolerance is useful for each your garden's health and seed conservation. Disease-resistant plant life are more likely to provide healthful seeds that might resist commonplace lawn disturbing situations.

Variety Research: Before choosing a plant for conservation, research its infection resistance tendencies. Varieties bred for resistance to precise diseases can contribute to your garden's conventional health and sturdiness.

6. Adaptable and Climate-Resilient Plants

Climate trade poses big demanding situations to gardeners. When choosing flowers for seed conservation, hold in mind those which might be adaptable to changing weather styles, temperature fluctuations, and unpredictable developing conditions.

Local Adaptation: Choose plant life which can be recognised to thrive on your unique weather. They have likely advanced genetic inclinations that assist them resist community weather extremes and seasonal fluctuations.

Crop Wild Relatives: Investigate crop wild circle of relatives, which can be frequently more adaptable and resilient. These vegetation can be property of precious genetic cloth for breeding programs and future conservation efforts.

7. Record Keeping

Accurate document-preserving is important for a success seed conservation. Keeping certainly one of a type facts of the plant life you're keeping will assist you tune the statistics and usual overall performance of every variety.

Data to Record: Document the variety, deliver, planting date, and any precise traits or traits of the plants you are holding. Note any changes or variations placed within the vegetation over the years.

Labeling and Organization: Use easy and durable labels to tag each plant or variety. Organize your statistics to ensure you could hint the statistics and not unusual overall performance of the seeds you are saving.

8. Seed Harvesting and Storage

Proper seed harvesting and garage are vital to keep seed viability through the years. Learn the techniques for harvesting and storing seeds from top notch plant species to ensure their lengthy-term protection.

Dry and Store Seeds: After harvesting seeds, make certain they may be very well dried to prevent mold and sickness. Store seeds in airtight bins in a groovy, darkish, and dry area. Include moisture-absorbing packets to lessen humidity degrees inside garage packing containers.

Regular Viability Testing: Periodically take a look at the viability of your stored seeds to ensure they remain viable. If vital, refresh your seed collection via sowing and saving seeds from the following vegetation.

9. Sustainable Practices

Sustainable gardening practices amplify to seed conservation efforts. As you embark on your seed-saving adventure, take into account ethical and sustainable practices, together with the following:

Avoid Overharvesting: When saving seeds from wild or local vegetation, avoid overharvesting to make sure their extended-term survival in natural habitats.

Promote Open-Pollination: Encourage open-pollination and genetic variety within your garden. Open-pollinated vegetation create numerous gene swimming pools that might advantage future conservation efforts.

Community Involvement: Collaborate with neighborhood gardening corporations or seed-saving organizations to alternate statistics, seeds, and belongings. Collective efforts can make a contribution to a broader variety of conserved plant sorts.

10. Sharing and Preservation

Seed conservation isn't best approximately safeguarding seeds to your private use but additionally about preserving and sharing plant sorts with the wider community. Consider the subsequent steps:

Community Seed Libraries: Support or set up network seed libraries to alternate and percentage seeds with fellow gardeners. These obligations sell neighborhood biodiversity and conservation efforts.

Collaboration with Seed Banks: Explore collaborations with seed banks and businesses that target retaining and sharing plant genetic variety on a larger scale.

Educational Outreach: Educate others approximately the importance of seed conservation and encourage them to take part in maintaining plant kinds.

Identifying Healthy Plants and Those to Avoid

Creating a thriving lawn starts offevolved with the selection of wholesome flora and a cautious method to the ones that would deliver issues.

When you may understand the signs and signs and signs and symptoms of a active, disease-loose plant in preference to 1 this might be tough, you will be nicely to your manner to a garden that prospers.

Identifying Healthy Plants

1. Strong Roots

Healthy plant life frequently have robust root structures. When shopping for potted plant life, gently slide the plant out of its pot to look at the roots. Look for white or moderate-coloured, organization, and properly-branched roots. Avoid vegetation with brown or easy roots, as they'll be laid low with root rot or extremely good sicknesses.

2. Vibrant Foliage

Healthy plants boast lush and colorful foliage. Leaves want to be green, till the plant naturally has a taken into consideration one among a type shade, and unfastened from discoloration, spots, or holes. Signs of healthy leaves encompass turgidity, uniform colour, and a clean appearance.

three. No Signs of Pests

Inspect plant life for any visible signs and symptoms and signs and symptoms of pests, alongside aspect chewed leaves, sticky residue (honeydew), or the presence of bugs. Healthy vegetation are commonly pest-free, so keep away from humans with any seen infestations.

four. Disease-Free Appearance

Healthy flora want to be unfastened from seen signs of diseases, along with wilting, rotting, or mould. Be mainly cautious of plant life with darkish spots, lesions, or bizarre growths, as those can be signs and symptoms of fungal or bacterial infections.

5. Balanced Growth

Healthy flowers display balanced increase, without a excessive leggy stems, elongated internodes, or stunted growth. Look for compact, hairy flora with well-proportioned foliage.

6. Healthy Stems

Examine the stems for any signs of illness or damage. Healthy stems are organization and unfastened from wounds, cankers, or discoloration. Avoid flowers with soft or discolored stems, as those can be suffering or inflamed.

7. Free-Flowing Sap

Healthy vegetation want to produce smooth, smooth sap even as lessen or pruned. If you take a look at discolored, foul-smelling, or oozing sap, it is able to recommend a problem in the plant.

eight. Strong Aroma (for herbs and fragrant flora)

Plants like herbs and aromatic species want to have a sturdy, feature aroma. Gently rub a leaf or stem among your fingers and be aware of the scent. A sturdy, tremendous aroma is indicative of a wholesome plant.

Identifying Plants to Avoid

1. Signs of Disease

Plants that exhibit visible signs and symptoms of disease, consisting of wilting, mildew, or discolored foliage, need to be averted. These signs and symptoms can indicate an risky plant that may introduce ailments in your garden.

2. Weak or Leggy Growth

Plants with inclined, leggy growth may additionally moreover conflict to thrive on your lawn. They regularly lack the strength and energy needed to face up to pests and environmental stressors.

three. Pests or Pest Damage

Plants that show signs of pest infestations or have seen harm as a result of insects need to be prevented. Pests can unexpectedly propagate to extraordinary plants to your lawn.

four. Overcrowding or Poor Spacing

If plant life are overcrowded in their pots or planting beds, they may have to compete for resources like light, nutrients, and water. This opposition can result in stunted increase and reduced energy.

five. Discolored or Wilted Foliage

Plants with discolored or wilting foliage can be underneath strain or stricken by illnesses. Avoid plant life with yellowing, brown, or drooping leaves, as they may not recover resultseasily.

6. Poor Root Systems

Plants with prone or crowded root systems of their pots are more likely to war whilst transplanted. Avoid plant life with root-bound or poorly evolved roots.

7. Weak or Damaged Stems

Plants with willing, damaged, or discolored stems also can have structural issues that affect their commonplace fitness and growth. Avoid the ones flora to save you destiny issues.

8. Unpleasant Odor (for herbs and fragrant vegetation)

Some plants also can emit an unpleasant or musty smell whilst beaten or bruised. This can be a hallmark of disease or a kingdom of lousy fitness. Avoid plant life with foul or uncommon scents.

9. Unhealthy Soil

When buying potted flowers, check the soil within the box. Soil that smells foul, is overly wet, or consists of visible signs of mould or fungal growth is an indicator of an dangerous plant.

10. Non-Indigenous or Invasive Species

Plants that aren't local on your location may also additionally require immoderate care and upkeep to thrive. They also can become invasive and damage local ecosystems. Avoid planting non-indigenous or invasive species except you are devoted to coping with them carefully.

eleven. Overly Mature or Leggy Transplants

Plants which might be too mature or leggy won't adapt nicely to transplanting. They may additionally additionally have hassle adjusting to new garden situations and might take longer to set up themselves.

## 12. Poorly Labeled or Misidentified Plants

Always be cautious when looking for flowers which are mislabeled or have unsure identification. Properly categorised plants make certain what you have become and that they will be appropriate for your lawn.

Chapter 4:

The Magical Moment - Seed Collection

Seed series is a pivotal second in the journey of nurturing your lawn and contributing to seed conservation efforts. This section will delivery you to the mystical worldwide of seed harvesting, wherein you can discover ways to recognize the right moments for series, recognize nature's indicators, and grasp the techniques and device needed to accumulate seeds successfully.

Waiting for the Right Moment: Nature's Harvesting Signals

Nature gives us with a wealth of scrumptious, nutritious, and sustainable food, but harvesting the bounty of the natural international requires staying electricity and a keen records of the symptoms and signs and symptoms and indicators it offers. Whether you are foraging inside the wild, tending to a lawn, or choosing fruit from trees, mastering to apprehend those cues is crucial for knowledge on the equal time as the instant is simply proper to accumulate your harvest.

1. Color Transformation

One of the maximum honest signs and symptoms of readiness for harvesting is a exchange in shade. Many end result, veggies, or maybe nuts undergo a alternate in colour as they ripen. Here are a few examples:

Fruit Ripening: Fruits like tomatoes, strawberries, and bananas flip colorful pink or yellow even as they are ripe and prepared to be picked. Others, like avocados, trade from inexperienced to a darkish purplish-black.

Observing the shade shift is a smooth sign that the fruit is ready for harvest.

Leafy Greens: Leafy greens, together with lettuce & spinach, are commonly harvested whilst their leaves are mild, younger, and colorful inexperienced. Once they start to yellow or become hard and sour, they're beyond their top.

2. Aroma and Fragrance

The aroma of a plant can be an remarkable indicator of readiness. Many quit result, herbs, and veggies emit a brilliant fragrance at the equal time as they may be at their pinnacle. For instance:

Herbs: Herbs like basil, mint, and cilantro release a sturdy, fragrant perfume while they'll be prepared to be picked. The aroma intensifies because the oils inside the leaves end up more focused.

Fruits: Fruits like melons, peaches, and pineapples emit a sweet, fragrant odor whilst completely ripe. If you could smell the fruit's natural fragrance, it's normally an terrific signal that it's far prepared to benefit.

three. Texture and Firmness

The texture and firmness of a plant can offer precious clues approximately its readiness for harvest:

Softness: Many end stop end result, like peaches, plums, and tomatoes, are prepared for harvest once they yield barely to moderate strain. If they sense too tough, they will be underripe, and if they may be tender, they may be overripe.

Crispness: Vegetables which incorporates cucumbers and snap peas must have a crisp, taut texture whilst they'll be at their height. When they come to be limp or rubbery, they're beyond their top.

four. Sound and Audible Cues

Some plant life provide audible cues to signal their readiness for harvest:

Audible "Pops": Popcorn, because of the fact the call suggests, produces an audible "pop" whilst the kernels are equipped to acquire. This takes vicinity at the same time as the moisture within the kernel turns to steam, inflicting it to burst open.

Crackling Seeds: Certain seeds, like sunflowers and beans, produce a crackling or rustling sound even as they may be dry and equipped to be harvested.

five.  Seed Dispersal

For plant life that produce seeds, their approach of seed dispersal can be a smooth indication of while it's time to gain:

Dandelions: Dandelion seeds are connected to fluffy, white pappus (the "parachutes" linked to the seeds) that enables them drift away within the wind. When the pappus is absolutely fashioned, it is a sign that the seeds are mature and prepared for series.

Dry Seed Heads: Many plant life, like basil or cilantro, produce seed heads that flip brown and dry as they mature. When those heads are geared up to shatter and launch their seeds, it's time to attain them.

6. Taste Testing

In some instances, the first-class way to affirm that a plant is prepared for harvest is to flavor it. This is mainly actual for culmination and veggies. For instance:

Berries: Many berries, which embody blueberries and blackberries, are at their sweetest and most flavorful at the equal time as they will be surely ripe. Taste-attempting out is frequently the most dependable approach for figuring out their readiness.

Root Vegetables: Root greens like carrots & beets can be dug up and tasted to gauge their sweetness and tenderness. If they taste properly, they will be equipped to be harvested.

7. Visual and Audible Clues within the Wild

Foraging in the wild calls for a keen eye and an records of herbal cues. Here are some extra signs to search for:

Seeds on the Ground: When you check seeds or nuts on the ground close to a tree or plant, it's far a signal that they will be possibly mature and equipped for harvesting. Squirrels and precise vegetation and fauna are remarkable foragers and can offer perception into the timing of a plant's adulthood.

Bird Activity: Birds are also professional foragers and may clue you in on the readiness of superb end result. If you word birds flocking to a tree or bush, it's far a splendid sign that the culmination are ripe.

8. Patience and Observation

Sometimes, nature's alerts are diffused, and it takes time and near commentary to determine the proper 2d for harvesting. For instance:

Pomegranates: Pomegranates are ready for harvest when the pores and pores and skin turns a rich, deep pink, and the fruit feels heavy for its duration. However, the splendid manner to confirm readiness is with the resource of lowering a fruit open and examining the seeds. They need to be plump and juicy, not dry or faded.

Edible Mushrooms: Foragers must have a deep know-how of the precise species they are harvesting, as mushrooms have unique symptoms of adulthood and aren't constantly apparent. Gills, spore colour, and cap duration are all crucial indicators.

nine. Local Wisdom and Seasonal Timing

In many regions, neighborhood statistics and traditions play a crucial characteristic in figuring out the proper time for harvesting. People who have lived in a particular region for generations regularly have treasured insights into the seasonal cues and community focus associated with harvesting.

10. Sustainability and Respect for Nature

While it's far vital to have a look at the symptoms and symptoms and alerts of readiness for harvesting, it's miles similarly important to acquire this with respect and sustainability in mind. Overharvesting or disrupting natural ecosystems can harm the environment and future foraging possibilities.

Techniques and Tools for Effective Collection

Collecting flowers, whether or not foraging in the wild or harvesting from your garden, requires a aggregate of strategies and tool to make certain success. Proper series strategies now not only maximize the yield however additionally sell sustainability and reduce harm to the surroundings.

Foraging inside the Wild

Foraging involves gathering stable to eat or beneficial flora from herbal environments. To do this ethically and correctly, undergo in mind the following strategies and gear:

1. Plant Identification

Before you gather any plant, it is crucial to correctly discover it. Mistakenly gathering poisonous plant life may be volatile, so spend money on challenge publications, apps, or are seeking out recommendation from experts to boom your identity abilities. Always be a hundred% notable about a plant's identification in advance than harvesting.

2. Sustainable Harvesting

Sustainability is high in foraging. Follow those hints to ensure you go away minimum effect:

Take Only What You Need: Harvest simplest what you could use, and keep away from gathering flora which can be unusual or inclined. Leave the majority of the population intact to make sure the plant's survival.

Use Scissors or Pruners: When harvesting wild plants, use scissors or pruners to lessen the plant cleanly, minimizing harm to the roots and surrounding vegetation.

Avoid Overharvesting: Do not select each plant of a species you come upon. Leave some inside the returned of to permit the population to regenerate.

3. Harvesting Tools for Wild Foraging

Carry the right tools to make certain effective and sustainable harvesting:

Scissors or Pruners: These equipment allow precise cuts without damaging the plant.

Small Basket or Bag: A moderate-weight area for gathering your harvest with out crushing the plant life.

Field Guide or Smartphone App: For plant identity in the place.

Gloves: To shield your arms from thorns, stinging flowers, or irritants.

Gardening and Cultivation

Harvesting from your lawn or cultivated flora calls for unique strategies and equipment for green collection. Here are some key issues:

1. Proper Timing

Timing is important for harvesting lawn vegetation. Different plants have awesome ranges of maturity at the same time as they'll be at their height for flavor and satisfactory. Here are some examples:

Tomatoes: Harvest even as they will be virtually ripe, as indicated with the aid in their colourful color and moderate softness whilst gently squeezed.

Herbs: Harvest leafy herbs like basil and cilantro truly earlier than they flower for the maximum immoderate flavor.

Root Vegetables: Dig up root greens like carrots and potatoes after they have reached the desired duration but earlier than they grow to be overgrown.

2. Harvesting Tools for Gardening

Having the right device makes harvesting greater green and lots less unfavourable in your flora:

Pruners or Shears: For easy cuts on stems, branches, or massive fruits.

Hand Trowel or Shovel: To carefully dig up root vegetables and exceptional plant life.

Harvesting Knife or Scissors: Ideal for delicate plant life like lettuce or herbs.

Picking Baskets or Containers: To collect and delivery your harvest without causing damage.

3. Proper Handling

Once you have got harvested your lawn vegetation, managing them cautiously is important to keep their wonderful:

Handle with Care: Treat your vegetation gently to keep away from bruising or harm. For end result and vegetables, use padded containers to prevent them from getting squashed or broken in the route of shipping.

Keep it Clean: Ensure your arms, system, and containers are smooth to prevent contamination and the spread of pathogens.

4. Sustainable Gardening Practices

Gardening practices also can promote sustainability within the lawn:

Crop Rotation: To prevent soil depletion & pest assemble-up, rotate plant life annually.

Composting: Recycle plant waste by the usage of turning it into compost, enriching your soil for destiny vegetation.

Water Management: Use green watering techniques, like drip irrigation, to maintain water and decrease waste.

five. Seed Saving

For gardeners interested by sustainable practices, saving seeds is an critical approach:

Selecting Healthy Plants: Save seeds from the healthiest, maximum lively vegetation that show off perfect dispositions.

Proper Drying and Storage: Ensure that seeds are truely dry before storing them in a groovy, dark, and dry place.

Record Keeping: Maintain clean records of the seeds you keep, on the facet of range, supply, and any precise tendencies.

Pollination Management: To prevent skip-pollination and keep seed purity, positioned into effect isolation techniques whilst saving seeds from go-pollinated plants.

6. Continuous Monitoring

In each foraging and gardening, non-forestall tracking is pinnacle:

Watch for Pests & Diseases: Check your plant life on a ordinary foundation for any symptoms and signs and symptoms and symptoms of sickness or damage due to pests. Early discovery makes it possible to take preventative measures closer to infestations in addition to the spread of illness.

Check Maturity: Monitor the adulthood of your plants, so you harvest them at the right time. Some end end result and greens can ripen unexpectedly, and missing the proper harvest window can result in a lack of exceptional.

## 7. Ethical Considerations

Whether you're foraging inside the wild or harvesting from your lawn, moral problems are essential:

Leave No Trace: When foraging in the wild, leave nature as you positioned it. Avoid trampling flora or disturbing flowers and fauna.

Protect Pollinators: In your garden, create a pollinator-pleasant surroundings to useful aid bees and extremely good beneficial insects. Avoid the use of risky pesticides.

Biodiversity: In both foraging and gardening, promote biodiversity. Grow some of plant species to beneficial useful resource ecological health and meals variety.

## eight. Sharing and Community

Both foragers and gardeners can gain from sharing understanding and tales:

Foragers' Groups: Join close by foragers' corporations to change information about excessive foraging places and plant identification.

Community Gardening: Collaborate with network gardening agencies to percentage gardening information and assets.

Chapter 5:

Treasures in a Box - Conservation and Care

Once you have got skilled the magical moment of seed series and accumulated the end result of your gardening efforts, it is time to defend the ones treasures in a discipline, making sure the safety of their energy and genetic variety. This phase will manual you via the publish-harvest routine, which include the important steps of cleansing, drying, and storing seeds, and show the secrets and techniques and techniques and strategies to retaining their prolonged-term strength.

Post-Harvest Routine: Cleaning, Drying, and Storing Seeds

Once you've efficaciously harvested seeds from your lawn or foraged them from the wild, the following critical step is to ensure their prolonged-term viability through nicely cleaning, drying, and storing them. Proper placed up-harvest care not most effective continues the tremendous of the seeds however moreover extends their shelf lifestyles.

Cleaning Seeds

Cleaning seeds is step one within the post-harvest everyday. It receives rid of any very last plant material, particles, or contaminants from the seeds. This now not simplest improves seed storage but additionally reduces the threat of pathogens or mold growing on the seeds. Here's a way to easy seeds effectively:

Supplies You'll Need:

A sieve or strainer with considered one of a kind-sized shows to break up seeds from particles.

A shallow dish or tray for sorting seeds.

A bucket or subject for containing the seeds.

Clean water for rinsing.

Steps for Cleaning Seeds:

1. Collect Seeds: Start through amassing the seeds you want to clean. These can be seeds from harvested stop end result, vegetables, herbs, or foraged flora.

2. Remove Excess Debris: Initially, pick out out any huge debris like leaves, stems, or twigs via hand. A slight shake or tapping the plant cloth over a tray can help dislodge seeds.

three. Rinse Seeds: In a few cases, rinsing seeds can be useful. Submerge the seeds in smooth, cool water, and use your palms to gently rub the seeds and separate them from clinging particles.

four. Use a Sieve: To similarly separate seeds from plant material, pass them via a sieve or strainer. Select a sieve with the right-sized mesh to permit seeds to pass thru even as trapping larger particles.

5. Sort Seeds: After sieving, switch the seeds to a shallow dish or tray. Inspect them cautiously for any ultimate plant fabric, and remove it by way of hand.

Drying Seeds

Drying is a essential step to reduce the moisture content cloth in seeds, that is important for stopping mold and retaining seed viability. The drying approach want to be accomplished with care to save you any harm to the seeds. Here's the manner to dry seeds correctly:

Supplies You'll Need:

A tray, plate, or dish for spreading seeds in a unmarried layer.

A nicely-ventilated, dry, and dark vicinity.

Steps for Drying Seeds:

1. Spread Seeds in a Single Layer: After cleaning, spread the seeds in a unmarried layer on a tray, plate, or dish. This guarantees even drying and prevents seeds from clumping collectively.

2. Choose a Suitable Location: Place the tray in a properly-ventilated vicinity, some distance from direct sunlight, in a dry and dark environment. The seeds ought to be blanketed from moisture and humidity.

three. Allow Adequate Time: The drying machine can take everywhere from a few days to a few weeks, depending on the seeds' duration and moisture content. Be patient and make certain that the seeds are absolutely dry in advance than proceeding to the subsequent step.

4. Test for Dryness: To take a look at if the seeds are dry, squeeze some seeds amongst your thumb and forefinger. If they sense tough, brittle, and do not bend, they may be correctly dried.

Storing Seeds

Storing seeds properly is the vital component to keeping their viability and ensuring a achievement germination inside the destiny. The intention is to defend the seeds from moisture, pests, and temperature fluctuations. Follow the ones steps for storing seeds:

Supplies You'll Need:

Small, hermetic containers or seed envelopes.

Silica gel packets or rice for moisture control.

A cool, dark, and dry garage vicinity.

Steps for Storing Seeds:

1. Use Appropriate Containers: Transfer the without a doubt dried seeds to small, hermetic containers, like glass jars, or seed envelopes. Make certain the packing containers are smooth and dry.

2. Label the Containers: Label each container with the call of the seed range and

the date it become harvested. This enables you maintain track of the seeds and their age.

3. Add Moisture Control: To save you moisture buildup in the boxes, encompass moisture-soaking up packets or area a few grains of rice in a fabric bag. These assist preserve the seeds' moisture content at an appropriate degree.

four. Store in a Cool, Dark, and Dry Place: Choose a fab, dark, and dry place for storing seeds. A basement, pantry, or refrigerator may be suitable. Avoid exposing seeds to direct daylight or temperature fluctuations.

five. Regularly Check Seeds: Periodically check your stored seeds for signs and symptoms and symptoms of moisture or pests. If you test any issues, cope with them proper now to make certain the seeds stay in appropriate scenario.

Additional Tips for Successful Seed Storage:

Use Airtight Containers: Airtight containers are important for stopping moisture and pests from infiltrating your seed storage.

Optimal Temperature: Store seeds at temperatures round 40°F (four°C) or slightly cooler. This permits hold their viability.

Avoid Freezing: While cooler temperatures are excellent, avoid freezing seeds, as it may harm them.

Test Germination: Periodically take a look at the germination rate of stored seeds to make certain their viability. To do this, place a few seeds in a moist paper towel and take a look at their germination rate over a week.

Rotate Seeds: To hold seed viability, rotate your stored seeds through the use of the oldest ones first and changing them with freshly harvested seeds.

Maintain Records: Keep real facts of your seed storage, which encompass the seed types, dates, and situations, that will help you track seed longevity and viability.

Share Your Seeds: Consider sharing your seeds with close by seed libraries or gardening businesses to sell biodiversity and seed-saving efforts.

Secrets to Preserving Seed Vitality

Seeds are the lifeblood of a sustainable garden, and their power is paramount for successful gardening endeavors. Preserving seed power ensures that your garden continues to thrive and offer bountiful harvests one year after year.

1. Select Healthy Plants

The first secret to maintaining seed electricity is first of all healthful flora. By choosing robust, sickness-resistant, and well-tailored plant types, you lay the basis for strong and critical seeds. Here's a way to do it:

Choose Open-Pollinated Varieties: Select open-pollinated or heirloom plant types every time viable. These vegetation normally generally tend to provide seeds with genetic variety and adaptableness.

Avoid Inbred or Weak Plants: Be selective to your breeding selections, keeping off vegetation that display signs and symptoms of inbreeding despair, disease susceptibility, or weak factor.

2. Isolate Crops for Pure Seeds

Cross-pollination can cause hybridization and decrease seed purity. To preserve seed energy and hold the traits of specific plant sorts, it is critical to prevent bypass-pollination. Here's how to attain that:

Plant Separation: Plant superb styles of the equal species as an extended way aside as their unique pollination dreams require. Consult reliable assets for endorsed isolation distances.

Hand-Pollination: In some times, you could manually pollinate plants to make certain pure seed production. Use small paintbrushes or cotton swabs to transfer pollen amongst vegetation.

Time-Based Planting: Stagger the planting instances of associated kinds to restriction the possibilities of them flowering simultaneously.

three. Practice Proper Seed Saving Techniques

The manner you acquire and keep seeds notably affects their power. Follow these extraordinary practices for seed saving:

Harvest at Peak Maturity: Collect seeds from flowers at their top maturity. This ensures that the seeds have evolved fully and are prepared for garage.

Clean Seeds Thoroughly: As stated in a previous segment, properly clean the seeds to cast off any plant debris, as this may sell mould or pests.

Dry Seeds Adequately: Ensure that the seeds are thoroughly dry in advance than storing them. Incomplete drying can reason mold boom and decreased energy.

Store in Cool, Dry, and Dark Conditions: Maintain seeds in a groovy, darkish, and dry surroundings to prevent them from turning into dormant or dropping strength.

4. Maintain Records

Keeping precise statistics of your seed-saving efforts is a thriller to retaining seed power. This exercising allows you to song the fulfillment of severa types and guarantees you don't forget important details. Record the following:

Variety Names: Document the names of the plant types you're developing and saving seeds from.

Harvest Dates: Note the dates even as you gathered the seeds. This permits you gauge their age.

Isolation Practices: Keep statistics of ways you isolated vegetation to prevent bypass-pollination.

Seed Storage Details: Include records about in which and the manner you saved the seeds.

Germination Rates: After a duration, test the germination costs of your stored seeds to ensure their viability.

Successes and Failures: Don't shy away from documenting each a success and unsuccessful attempts at seed saving. This statistics can help you have a examine out of your tales.

5. Encourage Biodiversity

A severa lawn is a healthful lawn. Biodiversity strengthens ecosystems and promotes natural pest manipulate on the equal time as additionally improving seed electricity. Here's the way to encourage biodiversity on your garden:

Plant a Variety of Species: Cultivate a big range of plant species in your garden. This variety attracts a broader spectrum of beneficial bugs and pollinators.

Support Native Plants: Incorporate neighborhood plant species into your garden layout. They are properly-best for your community weather and might make contributions to seed banks for conservation.

Create Habitats: Design your garden to offer habitats for herbal global, collectively with birdhouses, bee-friendly vegetation, and water sources.

6. Share and Exchange Seeds

Seed sharing and change is a powerful mystery to preserving seed energy. By collaborating in nearby seed exchanges or sharing seeds with fellow gardeners, you are making contributions to maintaining genetic range and selling healthful seeds. Consider the ones steps:

Join a Seed Library: Many groups have seed libraries in which you can borrow seeds, develop them, keep some, and pass lower back the saved seeds to the library for others to apply.

Participate in Seed Swaps: Attend nearby seed swaps or exchanges to diversify your seed series and have interaction with different like-minded gardeners.

Connect with Gardeners: Form connections with different gardeners and trade seeds informally to make bigger the genetic range on your garden.

7. Embrace Organic and Sustainable Gardening Practices

Preserving seed vitality is going hand in hand with sustainable and natural gardening practices. By prioritizing the fitness of your soil, minimizing pesticide use, and using natural fertilizers, you create an environment in which seeds can thrive. Embrace those sustainable practices:

Composting: Recycle plant waste and kitchen scraps into compost to enhance your soil virtually.

Crop Rotation: Change the vicinity of plants each season to lessen the risk of soilborne illnesses and enhance soil fitness.

Integrated Pest Management (IPM): Use IPM strategies to reduce using chemical pesticides and prioritize natural pest control strategies.

Cover Cropping: Plant cover plant life at a few diploma in the off-season to decorate soil shape and upload nutrients to the soil.

Soil Testing: Regularly test your soil to assess nutrient ranges and pH, and amend it as wanted.

8. Continue Learning

The final thriller to keeping seed energy is a commitment to non-forestall analyzing. Gardening is a dynamic and ever-evolving journey. Stay informed about the extremely-modern-day practices, make bigger your skills, and in no manner save you exploring new strategies to decorate your lawn and maintain seed strength.

Join Gardening Organizations: Many gardening corporations provide property, workshops, and educational possibilities for gardeners the least bit degrees.

Read Books and Journals: Stay updated with gardening literature and journals to get entry to precious insights and techniques.

Attend Workshops and Conferences: Participate in gardening workshops, seminars, and conferences to check from professional gardeners and specialists.

Sowing the preserved seeds marks the start of a brand new cycle on your gardening adventure. This segment will guide you through the method of records the most effective timing and techniques for planting preserved seeds, in addition to the critical practices for being concerned and nurturing your developing flowers.

Following the Seasons: When and How to Plant Preserved Seeds

Preserving seeds is handiest the first step in a gardener's adventure closer to sustainability. The next crucial section is planting those seeds at the right time and in the right way to ensure a a success lawn. Understanding your neighborhood climate, the best requirements of the flowers you're developing, and the cycles of nature is important for powerful seed sowing.

1. Know Your Growing Zone

Every vicinity has a completely precise weather, and expertise your nearby developing zone is the first step in figuring out even as to plant your preserved seeds. The USDA Plant Hardiness Zone Map is a treasured useful resource for gardeners inside the United States, whilst similar maps are available for awesome regions. Identify your growing sector, because it will assist you pick out the right planting times and suitable plant sorts.

2. Choose the Right Season

Plants have particular developing seasons, and choosing the right time to plant your seeds is vital. Here's a breakdown of the seasons and whilst to plant your preserved seeds:

Spring: Many vegetable flora, on the facet of tomatoes, peppers, cucumbers, and beans, are normally sown within the spring while the risk of frost has handed, and the soil has warmed up. Early spring is also a incredible time for cool-season plant life like lettuce, spinach, and peas.

Summer: Some warm temperature-loving plants like corn, melons, and okra are planted within the early summer season at the same time as the soil is continually heat. If you have a quick developing season, starting those seeds indoors and transplanting them can help ensure a harvest.

Fall: In regions with moderate winters, you could plant a 2d spherical of cool-season vegetation like carrots, beets, and kale in overdue summer time or early fall. These flora can be harvested nicely into iciness.

Winter: In temperate climates, a few hardy styles of vegetables and herbs can be sown immediately within the garden in overdue fall or early winter. While boom can also additionally sluggish inside the direction of the coldest months, the ones plant life can nonetheless thrive and offer sparkling produce.

3. Plan Your Planting Calendar

A planting calendar is a valuable device that will help you determine at the identical time as to sow your preserved seeds. Here's the manner to create a basic planting calendar:

Make a List: List the plant sorts you need to develop, which consist of their encouraged planting dates and days to maturity.

Work Backwards: Start together with your region's commonplace remaining frost date in the spring. Use this date as a reference point and paintings backward to determine at the identical time as to sow seeds interior or proper away in the garden.

Consider Succession Planting: Some plants may be planted more than one instances in a few unspecified time within the future of the season to growth the harvest. Plan successive plantings to ensure a non-stop supply of easy produce.

Include Fall Planting: If you recommend to plant a fall or iciness lawn, discover the notable dates for sowing seeds for the ones plants as well.

four. Indoor vs. Outdoor Sowing

Certain plant types advantage from being started out interior, on the equal time as others thrive while sown immediately within the garden. Here's a manner to determine which technique is excellent on your preserved seeds:

Indoor Sowing: Start seeds indoors for plant life that require an prolonged developing season, like tomatoes and peppers. This approach allows you to get a head start at the season. Utilize seed trays or pots full of seed-starting mixture, make sure proper moisture and mild, and switch the seedlings to the lawn even as the climate will become hotter.

Direct Sowing: Some plants, like beans, squash, and radishes, may be sown proper now within the garden. Choose a region with the proper soil temperature, and plant your seeds on the proper depth and spacing. Be exceptional to follow the pointers at the seed packets for each specific plant.

5. Prepare the Soil

The super of your lawn's soil is a big detail in a hit seed sowing. Ensure your garden beds have the proper conditions for plant increase:

Soil Testing: Conduct a soil take a look at to evaluate the pH, nutrient stages, and any deficiencies or imbalances to your soil. Amend the soil as had to create a fertile and balanced growing medium.

Prepare Garden Beds: Clear the garden bed of particles and weeds. Loosen the soil the use of a fork or tiller to create a crumbly texture, making it much less complex for younger roots to penetrate.

Compost and Mulch: Incorporate herbal rely like compost into the soil to beautify it with nutrients. Apply mulch on the soil surface to hold moisture and suppress weeds.

6. Follow Proper Plant Spacing and Depth

Planting intensity and spacing are essential factors in ensuring your preserved seeds germinate and make bigger properly:

Planting Depth: Check the seed packet for every plant range to determine the right planting depth. Some seeds have to be sown shallowly, on the same time as others require deeper planting.

Planting Spacing: Adequate spacing among plants is vital for actual air motion, lowering the threat of sickness and ensuring that each plant has room to develop. Adhere to the spacing suggestions supplied at the seed packet for correct plant placement.

7. Watering and Care

Young seedlings are sensitive, and right care is vital for his or her survival and increase:

Watering: Maintain everyday soil moisture with out overwatering. Utilize a mild spray or a soaker hose to save you disruption to the seeds or seedlings.

Thinning: If you have were given sown multiple seeds in the identical spot, skinny the seedlings once they emerge to make sure they've exact enough location to develop.

Fertilization: Apply herbal fertilizers or compost tea as had to offer essential nutrients for plant increase. Be careful not to over-fertilize, as this may harm flora.

eight. Pest and Disease Management

Gardens can entice pests and diseases that threaten your vegetation. Keep an eye out for any troubles and take movement to guard your lawn:

Companion Planting: Planting nice species collectively can help deter pests certainly. Research accomplice planting strategies to your unique plants.

Monitor for Signs of Problems: Check your plant life on a normal basis for any signs of illness or infestation. The potential to intrude fast way to in advance detection.

Organic Pest Control: Use herbal techniques to manipulate pests, which incorporates introducing beneficial bugs, like ladybugs, or the use of natural pesticides as a totally ultimate lodge.

Crop Rotation: Rotate flowers each season to minimize the chance of soilborne diseases and pests building up inside the soil.

nine.   Label and Record Keeping

To preserve an organized garden and make sure you understand what you've got planted wherein, use labels and keep correct statistics:

Plant Labels: Use plant labels or tags to mark the plants on your garden. Include the plant call, range, and planting date.

Record Keeping: Keep a gardening mag or spreadsheet to song your planting dates, types, and any issues or successes you stumble upon at some point of the season.

10. Embrace Patience and Observation

Gardening is a workout that calls for patience and eager remark. Allow your lawn to enlarge, analyze from your research, and make modifications as wanted. Nature will regularly offer cues and comments on a way to attend to your flowers.

Care and Nourishment: Monitoring Growth and Ensuring Plant Health

Once your seeds have germinated and greater youthful flowers have emerged, your role as a gardener shifts from sowing to nurturing. To sell robust boom and make certain the fitness of your plant life, you will need to display their progress and provide the care and nourishment they require.

1. Regular Inspection

Regular inspection of your lawn is a critical exercise to make sure plant health. By watching your plants carefully, you could trap issues early and take proactive measures. Here's what to look for:

Pest Damage: Check for signs and symptoms and signs of pests, which embody chewed leaves, holes, or discolored regions. Different pests depart specific marks.

Disease Symptoms: Look for symptoms and symptoms and symptoms of sickness, collectively with spots, wilting, yellowing, or uncommon increase patterns.

Weed Growth: Keep a watch constant constant on weed improvement, as they're capable of compete for property and host pests.

Nutrient Deficiencies: Pay hobby to any symptoms of nutrient deficiencies, like yellowing leaves (indicative of a nitrogen deficiency) or discolored leaf edges (indicative of a potassium deficiency).

2. Watering

Proper watering is essential for plant health. The proper quantity of water ensures that your flora accumulate the critical hydration and vitamins. Here are some watering recommendations:

Water at the Root Zone: Water the plant life immediately at their base to save you wetting the foliage, as this will probable bring about illness.

Deep Watering: Giving the soil an awesome soaking can foster deeper root improvement. A shallow watering pattern may additionally additionally bring about roots which are in addition shallow and fragile.

Consistency: Water constantly, aiming to hold a uniform degree of moisture. Prevent the soil from turning into excessively dry or waterlogged.

Morning Watering: Watering inside the morning lets in the vegetation to dry before nighttime, decreasing the risk of fungal ailments.

three. Fertilization

Plants require a balance of important vitamins to thrive. Soil attempting out and announcement can manual your fertilization practices:

Soil Testing: Conduct soil sorting out to determine out the quantities of vitamins and the pH of the soil. In mild of the findings, fertilizers and excellent styles of herbal be counted should be brought to the soil as essential.

Organic Fertilizers: Use herbal fertilizers like compost, nicely-rotted manure, and natural amendments to complement the soil with crucial vitamins.

Feeding Schedule: Develop a feeding time desk based mostly on the specific nutrient requirements of your vegetation. Different vegetation can also additionally want diverse nutrient ratios at first-rate growth ranges.

four. Pruning and Deadheading

Pruning and deadheading are important practices for controlling plant boom and selling flowering:

Pruning: Trim lower again overgrown branches and stems to hold the shape and period of your flowers. Pruning additionally encourages new boom and improves air bypass.

Deadheading: Remove spent flowers to stimulate the producing of latest blooms and save you flowers from setting strength into seed manufacturing.

www.ingramcontent.com/pod-product-compliance
Lightning Source LLC
Chambersburg PA
CBHW071446080526
44587CB00014B/2012